California ROCKS!

A Guide to Geologic Sites in the Golden State

KATHERINE J. BAYLOR

2010
Mountain Press Publishing Company
Missoula, Montana

Library of Congress Cataloging-in-Publication Data
Baylor, Katherine J., 1961–
California rocks! : a guide to geologic sites in the Golden State / Katherine J. Baylor.
p. cm.
Includes bibliographical references and index.
ISBN 978-0-87842-565-5 (pbk. : alk. paper)
1. Geology—California—Guidebooks. 2. California—Guidebooks. I. Title.
QE89.B39 2010
557.94—dc22
2010003529

Printed in Hong Kong by Mantec Production Company

Mountain Press Publishing Company
P.O. Box 2399 • Missoula, Montana 59806
(406) 728-1900

For my favorite young Californians:

Kira, Emily, Vanessa, and Ryan

PREFACE

California's high mountains, rocky coastlines, inland valleys, stunning beaches, and warm deserts draw visitors from around the globe. This spectacular tableau is the culmination of hundreds of millions of years of geologic processes, from the collision of tectonic plates to volcanic eruptions and earthquakes, to glaciation, sea level changes, erosion, and deposition. The reddish brown, tightly folded rock layers in Golden Gate National Recreation Area? Radiolarian chert. The cluster of peaks that rise out of the Central Valley north of Sacramento? A young volcano known as Sutter Buttes. The steeply tilted rock layers in Devils Punchbowl County Park? A syncline.

California has more than 25 national parks, 270 state parks, and countless hundreds of regional and local parks. In this book, I have summarized the geologic setting of 65 of the parks and special places statewide, with an emphasis on what is visible to the casual observer. The geologic summaries

in this book are intentionally short, and telling the complete geologic story of the Golden State is beyond the scope of this book. Readers searching for more in-depth discussion are encouraged to consult the section Further Reading, at the back of the book.

Although the sites listed in this book are nearly all accessible by paved roads, many are in relatively remote areas of California. Invest in high-quality road maps, and know how to use them. Members of the Automobile Association of America (AAA) will find the California "sectional" map series to be of a scale adequate to reach most of the sites listed in this book. Use computer-based mapping tools with caution.

Nearly every site listed in this book is a protected public space. National, state, and local parks strictly prohibit the collection of rocks, soil, and other natural features. Rock outcrops should be left in their natural state. Rock weathering is a natural process that adds to the beauty of the landscape.

ACKNOWLEDGMENTS

Many people contributed to the success of *California Rocks* by suggesting sites, reviewing specific sections, and providing photographs. I thank my editor at Mountain Press, Jennifer Carey, and the following individuals: Ken Aalto, Scott Anderson, John Arnold, Randy Bolt, Kristi Britt, Ed Clifton, Susan Davis, Carlos de la Rosa, Joel Despain, Jason DeWall, Julie Donnelly-Nolan, Steve Edwards, Will Elder, Chris Farrar, Cynthia Gardner, Eric Geist, David C. Greene, Don Grine, Ed Guaracha, Jane Hall, Karen Haner, John M. Harris, Lauren Harrison, Brian Hausback, Mark Jorgensen, Brian Ketterer, Kevin Key, Jody Kummer, Mark Langner, Ed Leong, Mary Maret, Dave Marquart, Seth Migdail, Ron Munson, Jeff Nickell, Juventino Ortiz, Charles Paull, Josh Pederson, Roi Peers, David Pryor, Linda Rath, Christina Sherr, Jeanne Sisson, Linda Slater, John Slenter, Doris Sloan, Woody Smeck, Dar Spearing, Bob Spoelhof, Miles Standish, Greg Stock, Phil Stoffer, Michael Strickler, Karl Tallman, Lindsey Templeton, Walter Vennum, Michael Walawender, Xiaoming Wang, Dave Whistler, Carol Witham, and Joe Zarki.

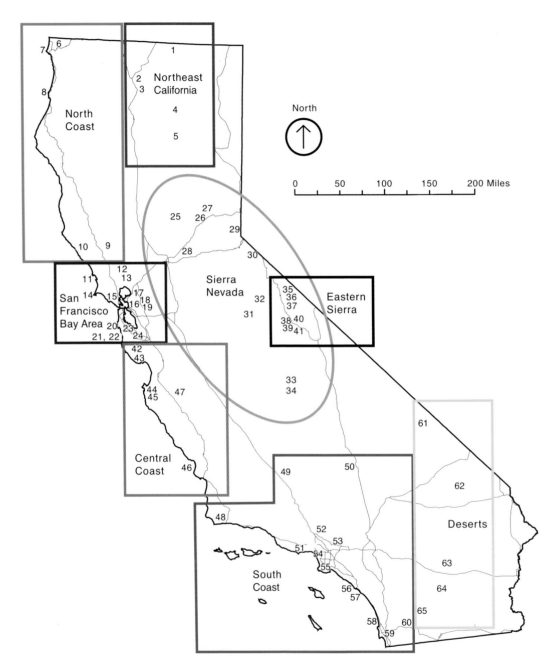

Regions in California Rocks. *Numbers correspond to specific sites.*

CONTENTS

Preface iv

Acknowledgments v

Geologic Time Scale ix

Plate Tectonics and California 1

Northeast California 5

  1. Lava Beds National Monument 6
     Caves in Basalt

  2. Mount Shasta 7
     A Stratovolcano

  3. Castle Crags State Park 8
     Exfoliation Joints in Granitic Rock

  4. McArthur–Burney Falls Memorial State Park ... 9
     A Spring-Fed Waterfall

  5. Lassen Volcanic National Park 10
     Eruptions and Boiling Springs

North Coast 13

  6. Jedediah Smith Redwoods State Park 14
     Josephine Ophiolite

  7. Crescent City 15
     Tsunami Country

  8. Patrick's Point State Park 16
     Franciscan Mélange and Younger Rocks

  9. Cache Creek Natural Area 17
     The Great Valley Sequence

  10. Salt Point State Park 18
     Trace Fossils

San Francisco Bay Area 20

  11. Sonoma Coast State Park 21
     Sea Stacks

  12. Calistoga's Petrified Forest 22
     Petrified Wood

  13. Napa Valley 23
     Terroir of Wine

  14. Point Reyes National Seashore 24
     The San Andreas Fault and the Rocks It Brought with It

  15. Golden Gate National Recreation Area ... 28
     Radiolarian Chert and Pillow Basalt

  16. Sibley Volcanic Regional Preserve 31
     Young Volcanics in the Coast Range

  17. Black Diamond Mines Regional Preserve ... 32
     California Coal

  18. Mount Diablo State Park 33
     Trail Through Time

  19. Vasco Caves Regional Preserve 34
     Concretions in Sandstone

  20. Mavericks Surf Break 35
     Seafloor Topography

  21. San Gregorio State Beach 36
     Sea Caves and Trace Fossils

  22. Bean Hollow State Beach 37
     Tafoni and Graded Bedding

  23. Los Trancos Open Space Preserve 38
     The 1906 Earthquake

  24. Almaden Quicksilver County Park 39
     Mercury Mine

Sierra Nevada 40

  25. Sutter Buttes 41
     A Young Volcanic Center

  26. Empire Mine State Historic Park 42
     Hard Rock Gold Mine

  27. Malakoff Diggins State Historic Park 43
     Hydraulic Mining of Placer Deposits

  28. Mather Regional Park 44
     Vernal Pools

  29. Lake Tahoe 45
     History of a Basin

30. Grover Hot Springs State Park 46
    Sierra Volcanics
31. California State Mining and Mineral Museum 47
    Gemstones and Gold
32. Yosemite National Park 49
    Sculpting by Water and Ice
33. Kings Canyon National Park 52
    Mineralogy of Granite
34. Sequoia National Park 53
    Caves in Marble

Eastern Sierra 54
35. Bodie State Historic Park 55
    Gold Mining Ghost Town
36. Mono Lake Tufa State Natural Reserve 56
    Pillars of Limestone
37. Panum Crater 57
    A Very Recent Eruption
38. Devils Postpile National Monument 58
    Columns in a Lava Flow
39. Horseshoe Lake 59
    Carbon Dioxide Tree Kill
40. Hot Creek Geological Site 60
    Hot Geysers in a Cold Creek
41. Convict Lake 61
    A Roof Pendant

Central Coast 62
42. Castle Rock State Park 63
    Tafoni Weathering of Sandstone
43. Natural Bridges State Beach 64
    Coastal Erosion
44. Carmel River State Beach 65
    Submarine Monterey Canyon
45. Point Lobos State Natural Reserve 66
    The Salinian Block and the Carmelo Formation
46. Morro Bay State Park 68
    A Line of Volcanic Plugs
47. Pinnacles National Monument 69
    A Volcano Split by the San Andreas Fault

South Coast 70
48. Gaviota State Park 71
    The Monterey Formation

49. Kern County Museum 72
    Black Gold
50. Red Rock Canyon State Park 73
    Miocene Fossils
51. Santa Monica Mountains National Recreation Area 74
    Transverse Ranges
52. Vasquez Rocks Natural Area 76
    Red Conglomerates and Fanglomerates
53. Devils Punchbowl County Park 77
    Folded and Faulted Rocks
54. La Brea Tar Pits 78
    Ice Age Fossils
55. Abalone Cove Shoreline Park 79
    Landslides
56. Crystal Cove State Park 80
    Marine Terraces
57. San Onofre State Beach 81
    Cristianitos Fault
58. Torrey Pines State Natural Reserve 82
    Sedimentary Features along the Beach Trail
59. Mission Trails Regional Park 84
    Mountain of Granite
60. Cuyamaca Rancho State Park 85
    Rocks of the Peninsular Ranges

Deserts 87
61. Death Valley National Park 88
    Salt Flats in a Closed Basin
62. Mojave National Preserve 92
    Sand Dunes and Volcanic Tuff
63. Joshua Tree National Park 94
    Rock Weathering
64. Salton Sea State Recreation Area 96
    A Saline Lake
65. Anza-Borrego Desert State Park 97
    Flash Floods

Glossary 99
Site Contact Information 103
Further Reading 107
Index 109

GEOLOGIC TIME SCALE

Eon/Era	Period	Epoch	Age	Events
CENOZOIC	QUATERNARY	Holocene	11,500 years ago	
CENOZOIC	QUATERNARY	Pleistocene		← Long Valley Caldera erupts 760,000 years ago. ← Sherwin Glaciation about 1 million years ago sculpts Sierra Nevada.
CENOZOIC	QUATERNARY		1.8 million years ago	
CENOZOIC	TERTIARY (Neogene)	Pliocene	5.3	← Uplift of modern Sierra Nevada begins, continuing today.
CENOZOIC	TERTIARY (Neogene)	Miocene	23.0	← Basin and Range Province begins forming.
CENOZOIC	TERTIARY (Paleogene)	Oligocene	33.9	← San Andreas Fault begins forming
CENOZOIC	TERTIARY (Paleogene)	Eocene	55.8	
CENOZOIC	TERTIARY (Paleogene)	Paleocene		
MESOZOIC	Cretaceous		65 million years ago	
MESOZOIC	Cretaceous		145	⎫ Granitic rock of the Sierra Nevada and Peninsular Range forms.
MESOZOIC	Jurassic		199	
MESOZOIC	Triassic			⎭
PALEOZOIC	Permian		251 million years ago	
PALEOZOIC	Permian		299	
PALEOZOIC	Pennsylvanian		318	
PALEOZOIC	Mississippian		360	
PALEOZOIC	Devonian		417	← Marine sediments of future Sevehah Cliff are deposited.
PALEOZOIC	Silurian		443	
PALEOZOIC	Ordovician		488	
PALEOZOIC	Cambrian		542 million years ago	
PRECAMBRIAN	Proterozoic Eon			← oldest rocks in California
PRECAMBRIAN	Proterozoic Eon		2.5 billion years ago	
PRECAMBRIAN	Archean Eon		4.0	
PRECAMBRIAN	Hadean Eon		4.6 billion years ago	← approximate age of Earth

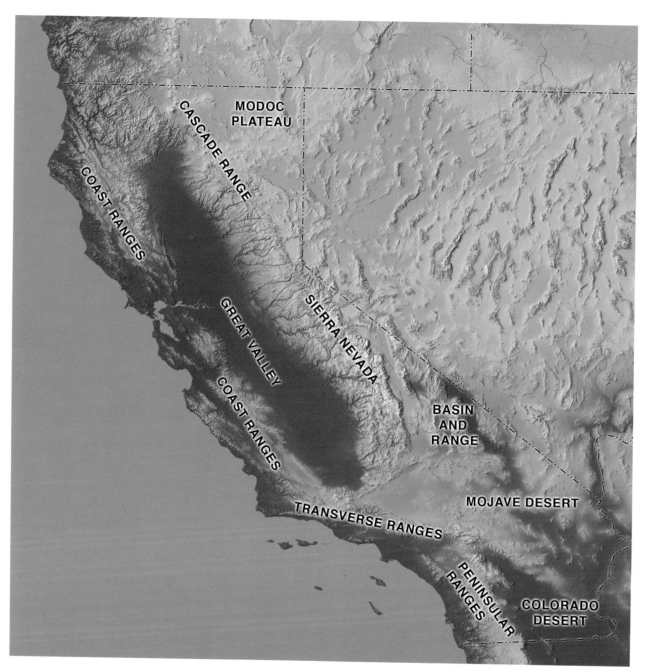

Geographic regions of California

PLATE TECTONICS AND CALIFORNIA

California's geologic history is best understood in the context of plate tectonics, a well-established theory developed in the 1960s. In the nineteenth century, earlier researchers, such as state geologist Josiah Whitney, were able to document the "what," but not the "why," of California's geologic landscape. Whitney, who led the first geologic survey of the state from 1860 to 1864, recognized the importance of fossils, sedimentary layers, and volcanic rocks in California's unique landscape but didn't have the tools to explain how all of the elements fit together. To fully appreciate the sites described in this book, you'll probably find it useful to understand the major elements of plate tectonics and how they help explain the California landscape.

The inner part of the Earth consists of a solid iron-nickel core surrounded by a liquid outer core. Above the core is the mantle, a thick semisolid layer that extends almost to Earth's surface. At the very surface of the Earth is the crust, a relatively thin layer of hard rock. Only about 3 miles thick in the deep ocean and more than 30 miles thick under high mountain ranges, the Earth's crust is broken into several large and many smaller pieces, called plates, that move slowly across the mantle. Plate tectonic movement is exceedingly slow, averaging inches per year. Over millions of years, however, the inches add up, leading to today's distribution of continents. Numerous lines of evidence support plate tectonic theory, including the presence of identical fossils on landmasses now separated by oceans, magnetic data from seafloor rocks, and geophysical information from earthquakes.

Boundaries between the Earth's plates take three general forms: divergent, convergent, and transform. Divergent plate boundaries occur primarily in the deep ocean, at seafloor spreading centers such as the Mid-Atlantic Ridge and

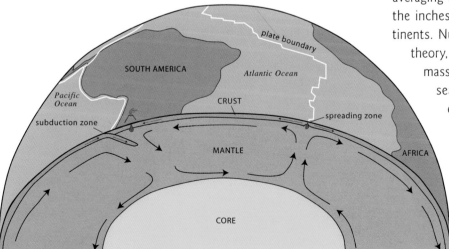

Cross section of the Earth —Modified from the U.S. Geological Survey

1

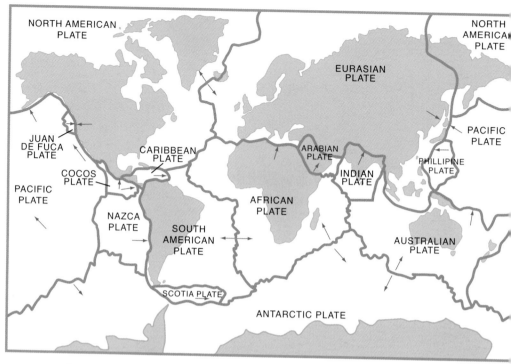

direction of plate movement

East Pacific Rise. These underwater mountain ranges, invisible to us until the development of sonar mapping technology, are zones of intense volcanic activity. New oceanic crust, primarily the volcanic rock basalt, is created at spreading centers.

Convergent boundaries form where collisions occur between two plates. At the collision site between an oceanic plate and a continental plate, oceanic crust, which is denser, is subducted beneath lighter continental rock and becomes incorporated into the mantle. Where two oceanic plates collide, generally the older plate, which is colder and denser, is subducted beneath the younger plate. In a few locations, most notably the Himalayas, continental crust from one plate converges with continental crust from another plate. At these convergences of two continental plates, neither plate is subducted, and the slow collision produces an ever-higher mountain range.

Subduction zones produce a great deal of heat, which melts the adjacent mantle rock and part of the down-going plate, forming magma. Magma that cools and solidifies deep underground forms granite and other intrusive igneous rocks. Magma that erupts from a volcano produces extrusive igneous rocks such as basalt or rhyolite.

The final type of plate boundary, and the most important type for many Californians, is the transform boundary, where two plates slide past each other. At a transform boundary, crust is neither created, as at a divergent boundary, nor destroyed, as at a convergent boundary, yet the forces involved are still extremely powerful and can reshape Earth's surface dramatically. California's mighty San Andreas Fault system, which extends approximately 800 miles from the Gulf of California to the Humboldt County coast, is a transform plate boundary where the Pacific Plate and North American Plate are moving slowly past each other. More than a single fault, the San Andreas system is a broad swath of related faults that take up stress at the boundary between the plates.

California's oldest rocks, in the state's southeastern deserts, are more than 1 billion years old, but rocks in most of the state's major landscape features, such as the Sierra Nevada and the Coast, Transverse, and Peninsular Ranges, began to form during the past 200 million years. Back then, the western edge of California was a convergent plate boundary where the dense oceanic Farallon Plate was subducted beneath the lighter continental North American Plate. Subduction provided heat energy that melted the overlying rock, which then cooled deep underground as granite along the eastern edge of California. The largest emplacement of granite, which occurred from about 210 to 80 million years ago, would become today's Sierra Nevada. At about the same time, granite and related igneous rocks of the Peninsular Ranges (primarily located in Riverside, Orange, and San Diego Counties) were also crystallizing deep underground.

The subducting Farallon Plate was also responsible for the formation of the rocks of California's Coast Ranges, which extend from near the California-Oregon border south to about San Luis Obispo. The dominant rock of the Coast Ranges is the Franciscan Complex, which includes deep oceanic floor rocks scraped off the descending Farallon Plate onto the edge of the North American Plate.

By about 30 million years ago, the Farallon Plate had been mostly subducted beneath the North American Plate. Riding behind the Farallon Plate was the Pacific Plate, which approached the North American Plate at an oblique angle, first touching North America at about present-day Los Angeles. As the Pacific Plate contacted the North American Plate, the boundary changed from subduction to transform movement. The nascent San Andreas Fault lengthened as more of the Pacific Plate contacted the North American Plate.

About 20 million years ago, tectonic stresses near the developing San Andreas Fault ensnared several large blocks of land near present-day San Diego. Over time, these blocks moved north and rotated until they were nearly transverse, or perpendicular, to the dominant northwest-southeast orientation of the Coast Ranges. These mountain blocks today form the Transverse Ranges of Santa Barbara, Ventura, and northern Los Angeles Counties.

Also starting about 20 million years ago, and roughly at the same time as the development of the San Andreas Fault system, the North American Plate underwent tectonic expansion across much of the western United States, including all of present-day Nevada and large parts of Utah, California, Arizona, and New Mexico. The large-scale stretching produced hundreds of extensional, or normal, faults across the region. The faulted blocks tilted up, forming the characteristic basin (valley) and range (mountain) topography seen in California's southeast deserts today. Extensional faulting was also responsible for uplift of the Sierra Nevada in the past few million years.

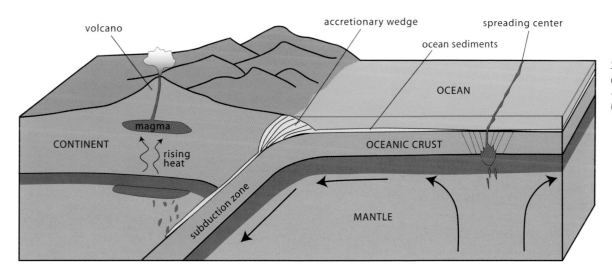

Subduction zone and spreading center —Modified from the U.S. Geological Survey

Uplift of the Sierra Nevada and many of the ranges within the Basin and Range Province continues today.

A small but tectonically significant remnant of the Farallon Plate remains today, in two portions: the Gorda Plate, offshore from Humboldt and Del Norte Counties in northern California, and the Juan de Fuca Plate, off the Oregon and Washington coast. Both are currently being subducted beneath the North American Plate. Heat energy from the subducting plates feeds the Cascade Range volcanoes, including Mount Shasta and Lassen Peak in California.

The Great Valley, more commonly known as the Central Valley, exists as a calm eye in the center of the geologic storm that defines the other provinces of California. This 400-mile-long plain bracketed by the Coast Range and the Sierra Nevada is a deep basin filled with tens of thousands of feet of sediment washed down from the mountain ranges that surround it. It's also California's most important agricultural area, producing almonds, walnuts, fruit, vegetables, and dairy products.

Plate boundaries on the west coast of North America

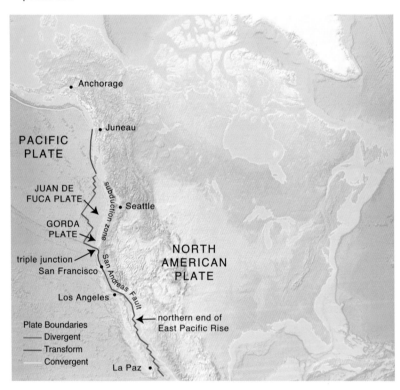

4

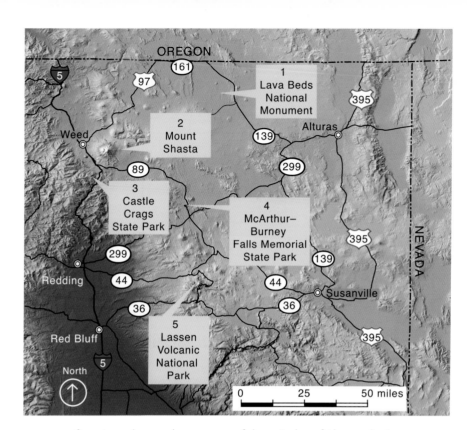

The map shows Northeast California with numbered points of interest:
1. Lava Beds National Monument
2. Mount Shasta
3. Castle Crags State Park
4. McArthur–Burney Falls Memorial State Park
5. Lassen Volcanic National Park

Cities: Weed, Redding, Red Bluff, Alturas, Susanville. Highways: 5, 97, 161, 139, 395, 299, 89, 44, 36. Labeled: OREGON, NEVADA.

North ↑

0 — 25 — 50 miles

NORTHEAST CALIFORNIA

Mount Shasta and Lassen Peak, both Cascade Range volcanoes, dominate the skyline in northeastern California. The Cascade Range volcanoes, which extend from California through Oregon and Washington and into British Columbia, have formed above the convergent plate boundary where the Gorda and Juan de Fuca Plates are being subducted beneath the North American Plate. Rising heat from the subducting plates provides the energy that fuels the volcanoes. Many of the prominent Cascade Range volcanoes, including Lassen Peak, Mount Shasta, Mount Baker, and Mount Rainier, are stratovolcanoes that tend to erupt explosively because the high silica content of their magma traps gas. The violent eruption on May 18, 1980, of Mount Saint Helens killed fifty-seven people and toppled or buried more than 200 square miles of

forest, and served as a powerful reminder of the explosive potential of the Cascade Range volcanoes.

The Modoc Plateau lava field, which lies east of Mount Shasta in far northeastern California, has an entirely different character. Unlike the explosive eruptions of silica-rich rhyolite magma from Lassen and Shasta, much of the lava of the Modoc Plateau consists of basalt, which is rich in iron and magnesium but relatively low in silica. As such, basalt lava erupts less explosively than rhyolite.

Medicine Lake Volcano, near the boundary of the Cascade Range and the Modoc Plateau, is a geological oddity that consists of a mix of basalt, andesite, and rhyolite lava. While the lower slopes are largely basalt, the upper reaches grade into andesite and rhyolite, which have a higher silica content. This indicates that several magma chambers of varying composition fed the volcano.

5

Skull Cave, a lava tube, in Lava Beds National Monument

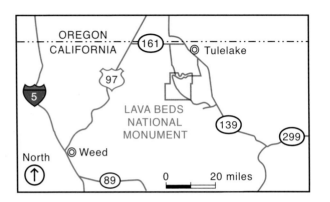

OREGON
CALIFORNIA
161
◎ Tulelake
97
5
LAVA BEDS
NATIONAL
MONUMENT
139
299
North
↑
◎ Weed
89
0   20 miles

1. LAVA BEDS NATIONAL MONUMENT
Caves in Basalt

Lava Beds National Monument is slightly off the beaten track, but the hundreds of caves in the lava make getting to this remote location near the Oregon border well worth the effort. The term *lava* is used for both the hot molten fluid that erupts from volcanoes and the hard basalt rock that cools from it. Lava tubes form when the surface of low-silica basaltic lava cools to a hard crust and the deeper, hotter lava continues flowing underneath. When the source of the magma stops producing lava but the hot lava inside the cooled crust continues to drain away, a hollow tube remains. Unlike limestone caves, which continue to develop, growing features such as stalactites and stalagmites, lava tubes are fully formed as soon as the lava hardens. Roof collapses of the hardened lava provide access to the caves. Individual caves are small segments of longer lava tubes that may stretch for miles. Most of the dozen or so lava tubes in the park originate at Mammoth Crater, a vent on the flank of Medicine Lake Volcano. This volcano, active for at least the past 700,000 years, is the product of crustal stretching. As the Earth's crust thins in

areas such as the Basin and Range Province, magma breaks through to form volcanoes.

To date, over eight hundred caves have been discovered at Lava Beds National Monument. Of these, approximately twenty are readily accessible to the public, but be forewarned: the caves range in height from walkable to only accessible by belly crawling, and most are head-bangers. Head protection is necessary. Mushpot, the only lighted cave, is located near the visitor center and has a paved floor and excellent descriptions of lava tube features. And while most of the caves dead-end after a few hundred feet, high-ceilinged Sentinel Cave runs for about half a mile and has entrances at both the upper and lower end. Slightly more challenging caves include Golden Dome and Sunshine, both of which require stooping in low spots. Some caves, such as the aptly named Catacombs and Labyrinth, are not suitable for inexperienced cavers because their many twists and turns can be disorienting. Skull Cave is among the park's few accessible ice caves. Water dripping down from the ground surface freezes in the cave in winter. The cave is situated in such a way that it traps cold air, allowing the ice to remain year-round.

Aerial view of Mount Shasta and Shastina from the west.
—U.S. Geological Survey, Cascades Volcano Observatory photo

2. MOUNT SHASTA
A Stratovolcano

Mount Shasta, the 14,163-foot-tall volcano that dominates the horizon in Siskiyou County, is the second highest in the Cascade Range; only Washington's Mount Rainier is higher. Mount Shasta has been erupting, on average, every 600 to 800 years for the past 10,000 years, and has an eruptive history that dates back some 600,000 years. Mount Shasta may have erupted as recently as 1786, as documented by the French explorer Jean-François de Galaup, comte de La Pérouse, when he was mapping the west coast of North America. Although he was far out to sea at the time, Mount Shasta is the only volcano that would have been in his line of sight. Limited field evidence on Mount Shasta supports the interpretation that there was a small eruption near the summit approximately 200 years ago.

Shastina, the prominent vent on the west slope of Mount Shasta, is about 9,500 years old. Both Shasta and Shastina are made of andesite and dacite, mid- to high-silica rocks typical of the high, steep stratovolcanoes common to the Cascade Range. The high silica content makes the lava very stiff, so it doesn't flow readily. Basalt lava, which is lower in silica and can flow long distances, typically forms lower-profile shield volcanoes, such as those found in Hawaii and at Medicine Lake Volcano, the source of the basalt lava field at Lava Beds National Monument. In a stratovolcano, multiple eruptions of lava and fragmental material build up over time.

The U.S. Geological Survey's Cascades Volcano Observatory monitors volcano-related activity near each volcano in the Cascade Range, including gas emissions, ground surface deformation, and earthquake activity. In the weeks and days prior to a volcanic eruption, the volcano may expand, magmatic gases are often detected, and earthquake intensity and frequency typically increase in response to magma rising toward the surface.

West side of Mount Shasta (high point at left) and Shastina (rounded dome at right)

Granitic spires in Castle Crags State Park. Castle Dome is the high, rounded peak in the center of the photograph.

3. CASTLE CRAGS STATE PARK
Exfoliation Joints in Granitic Rock

Castle Crags State Park and the adjacent Castle Crags Wilderness, about 50 miles north of Redding, encompass more than 14,000 acres of rugged peaks and conifer forests. Castle Crags is an odd island of granodiorite and trondhjemite, light-colored intrusive igneous rocks similar to granite, surrounded by a sea of Trinity Peridotite, an iron- and magnesium-rich igneous rock from the upper mantle. The peridotite, which is weaker and older (400 to 380 million years old) eroded faster than the intruding granodiorite (170 to 130 million years old), leaving the crags to stand out in a dramatic sawtooth profile. Over time, weathering has focused along joints, sets of planar fractures in the granodiorite. As the region was uplifted, the weathered rock eroded away, leaving behind the high spires and vertical rock walls. Another type of joint, called exfoliation joints, creates layers that look like an onion skin; these are responsible for the rounded shape of Castle Dome, one of the most prominent features of the park. Every now and then, an outer layer slides off with little or no warning. Despite the rockfall hazards, Castle Crags is a popular climbing spot, and its routes have imaginative names, such as "The Flying Monkey" and "Fist Fight with a Sumo Wrestler." The Pacific Crest Trail passes through the park, and the nearby town of Castella serves as a major resupply point for long-distance hikers—and a place where they can enjoy a hot shower and a taste of civilization before heading back out on the trail.

4. MCARTHUR–BURNEY FALLS MEMORIAL STATE PARK
A Spring-Fed Waterfall

Located midway between Lassen Peak and Mount Shasta, Burney Falls was long considered sacred by people of the Pit River Nation. European fur traders first arrived at the falls in the 1820s, and decades of conflict followed. Samuel Burney, a farm caretaker, was a victim of the conflict in the late 1850s. The park's other namesake, the McArthur family, owned 160 acres of land surrounding the falls, which they deeded to the state of California in 1920 for parkland.

Although other waterfalls are higher, Burney Falls is one of the most dramatic spring-fed falls in California. Springs occur where groundwater reaches the land surface. Here, the springs emanate from the middle of the Burney Falls cliff face and mix with surface water from Burney Creek, which is mostly spring-fed upstream of the falls. The upper part of the cliff face is made of Burney Basalt, which cooled from lava between 1.8 and 1 million years ago. The relatively young Burney Basalt, highly fractured and permeable, sits atop much older and less permeable volcanic and sedimentary rocks. Groundwater flows rapidly downward through the Burney Basalt until it reaches the older rock and is forced out of the cliff face at the boundary between the older and younger rock.

The Burney Falls overlook, just a few hundred feet from the main parking lot, provides a panoramic view of the 100-million-gallon-per-day torrent of water that gushes over the precipice year-round. From the overlook, the Falls Loop Trail descends to the foot of Burney Falls and then makes a short loop along both sides of Burney Creek before returning to the overlook.

Springs flowing from a rock layer in the middle of the cliff face at Burney Falls

9

Devastated Area, the site of the 1915 Lassen Peak eruption

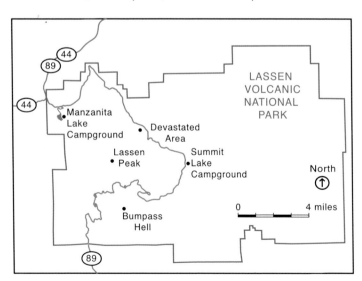

5. LASSEN VOLCANIC NATIONAL PARK
Eruptions and Boiling Springs

Lassen Peak is the southernmost volcano in the Cascade Range. The subduction of the Gorda Plate beneath the North American Plate continues to produce the heat that fuels the volcano and its hydrothermal areas. The Devastated Area in Lassen Volcanic National Park is a reminder of this active plate margin. A short loop trail that starts at the Devastated Area parking lot has a series of interpretative signs describing the eruptive events that occurred here from 1914 to 1921. In May of 1915, Lassen was visibly active, with more than 180 steam explosions blasting out of a 1,000-foot-wide crater. On the evening of May 14, incandescent blocks of lava bounced down the flanks of Lassen. On May 19, a mudflow produced by rapidly melting snow rushed 10 miles downslope. Finally, on May 22, an enormous eruption sent a column of volcanic ash 30,000 feet into the air, where it drifted as far as Winnemucca, Nevada, 200 miles to the east. The Devastated Area is littered with red and black boulders of dacite, a silica-rich volcanic rock that solidified from the lava erupted in 1915. The white speckles on the boulders are crystals of the mineral plagioclase. Hikers can get a spectacular view of the 1915 eruption area and surrounding volcanic landscape from the top of 10,457-foot Lassen Peak, but be forewarned: the trail climbs 2,000 feet in 2.5 miles.

Bumpass Hell, a 16-acre hydrothermal area in Lassen Volcanic National Park, was named for Kendall Vanhook Bumpass, a nineteenth-century explorer who promoted the area. As Bumpass led a group of visitors through the area, his leg plunged through the unstable ground into a boiling mud pool and was instantly scalded, giving the hydrothermal basin its name. Today, visiting Bumpass Hell is much safer—the National Park Service has constructed a sturdy boardwalk through the area, and visitors are warned to stay on it. The hydrothermal features, including fumaroles, mud pots, and boiling springs, are largely differentiated by their temperature and water content. Fumaroles, which are steam and volcanic gas vents, have the least water. More water and a bit of time produces a boiling mud pot, and even more water creates a boiling spring. The hydrothermal area is only a 1.5-mile hike from the parking lot on a moderate up-and-down trail, but visitors from sea level may find themselves breathing hard in the thin air at 8,000 feet elevation.

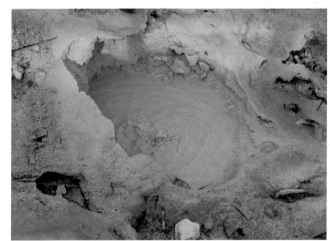

Boiling spring at Bumpass Hell

Bumpass Hell, a hydrothermal area in Lassen Volcanic National Park

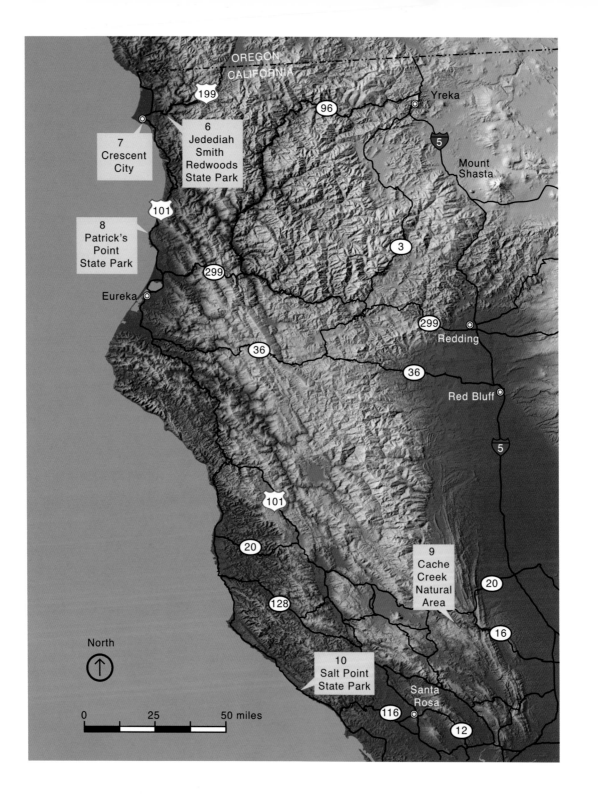

OREGON
CALIFORNIA

Yreka

199

96

5

6
Jedediah
Smith
Redwoods
State Park

Mount
Shasta

7
Crescent
City

101

3

8
Patrick's
Point
State Park

299

Eureka

299

Redding

36

36

Red Bluff

101

5

20

9
Cache
Creek
Natural
Area

128

20

16

North

↑

10
Salt Point
State Park

Santa
Rosa

0   25   50 miles

116

12

NORTH COAST

California's north coast is one of the most tectonically active areas of the state. The slow subduction of the Gorda Plate beneath the North American Plate results in earthquakes that serve as a constant reminder to residents that they live on the "ring of fire," the zone of volcanoes that borders the Pacific Plate. Although subduction, like all tectonic plate movement, averages only inches per year, stress on the plates can build up for many years until the plates suddenly shift several feet at once, causing earthquakes. Several large earthquakes have struck the north coast in recent decades, including a magnitude 7 temblor in 1992 that caused $48 million in damage and injured several hundred people.

The dominant rock unit of California's north coast, as well as much of the Bay Area and central coast, is the Franciscan Complex. This series of related oceanic rocks was accreted to the North American continent during the subduction of the old Farallon Plate. As the dense oceanic crust of the Farallon Plate descended beneath the lighter continental crust of the North American Plate, pieces of the Farallon Plate were scraped onto the continent, a process called accretion. The accretionary wedge includes basalt of the oceanic floor and vast amounts of sediment shed from the continent and deposited deep underwater. The major rock types in the Franciscan Complex include basalt, radiolarian chert, graywacke, and serpentinite.

Much of the basalt in the Franciscan Complex has pillows, indicating it cooled from lava that erupted underwater, which typically occurs at divergent plate boundaries or submarine volcanic vents. As hot lava erupts in the cold ocean, it is immediately quenched, forming a pillow-shaped blob of hardened lava. Radiolarian chert is a silica-rich rock composed almost entirely of radiolaria, a type of microscopic marine animal. Compaction of their silica skeletons over millions of years forms the rock. Franciscan graywacke is a sandstone with a mix of grain sizes deposited by turbidity currents, which are underwater landslides, sometimes triggered by earthquakes in the subduction zone. The bluish green rock serpentinite is altered peridotite, a rock from the upper mantle, the zone immediately below Earth's crust. The name *serpentine*, which is a mineral group, is often used for the name of the rock, which is California's state rock.

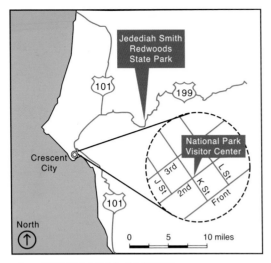

Cobbles at Jedediah Smith Redwoods State Park, many of which eroded from the Josephine ophiolite

6. JEDEDIAH SMITH REDWOODS STATE PARK
Josephine Ophiolite

With a watershed that covers more than 450 square miles and extends into southern Oregon, the Smith River's three forks and major tributaries drain parts of the Klamath, Siskiyou, and Coast Ranges. Although the Smith River is replete with whitewater rapids, it isn't necessary to kayak the entire river to explore the regional geology. Rocks from the upper reaches of the watershed tumble downstream in spring run-off and often eventually end up at Jedediah Smith Redwoods State Park. Speckled granite, striped metamorphic rocks, and a Hades rainbow of gray, black, and deep green rocks line the banks of the Smith River. Many of the black and greenish black rocks are derived from the Josephine ophiolite.

The name *ophiolite* doesn't designate a single rock type, but rather a specific sequence of rocks that represents the ocean floor formed at spreading centers. These deep ocean rocks, which are much denser than continental rock, such as granite, are normally subducted at convergent plate boundaries and only occasionally are accreted onto the continental margin. Ophiolites are a rare find, and the Josephine ophiolite, named for Josephine County, Oregon, is one of the most complete sequences ever documented.

The principal rock types found in an ophiolite sequence are, from bottom to top, peridotite, gabbro, sheeted dikes, and basalt. Peridotite is a very dense igneous rock that is formed in the upper mantle and composed almost entirely of the dark minerals pyroxene (black) and olivine (green). Smith River cobbles that are greenish black and seem very heavy for their size may be peridotite.

Gabbro, sheeted dikes, and basalt are magnesium- and iron-rich rocks that solidified from hot magma. What differentiates them is the degree of crystallization, with gabbro having the biggest crystals and basalt the smallest. Large crystals form in iron- and magnesium-rich magma that cools slowly deep underground, forming gabbro. In contrast, there is little time for crystals to form in lava that erupts from a volcano and cools quickly. At spreading centers, the magma moves to the surface along cracks. Sheeted dikes form when the magma solidifies in the cracks. Because the dikes are closer to the surface than the gabbro, the crystal size is intermediate between gabbro and basalt. Because lava erupting from an underwater volcanic vent is immediately quenched by seawater, it usually forms bulbous shapes known as pillow basalt, and these are a common feature in ophiolites.

7. CRESCENT CITY
Tsunami Country

In 1964 a massive undersea earthquake near Alaska triggered a tsunami that struck Crescent City. Large tsunamis, usually formed when a major earthquake produces a vertical displacement of the seafloor, are very rare events. The tsunami's destructive force isn't unleashed until it reaches shore. And contrary to the common conception, a tsunami that reaches land doesn't arrive as a single extraordinarily large wave, but rather as a series of incoming waves that may appear as individual floods of water. Depending on the shape of the coastline and the depth of the nearshore environment, the tsunami wave height may be magnified twentyfold or more, wreaking havoc on everything in its path.

The underwater topography near Crescent City is uniquely shaped to focus waves toward the town. As in many tsunamis, the first wave of the 1964 event was smaller than succeeding waves, which struck over the course of an hour. The third and fourth waves in the sequence were the largest and most destructive, estimated at more than 20 feet high. (The harbor wave gauge broke during the third wave.) The 1964 strike was by far the most destructive in Crescent City's recorded history, but more than two dozen small tsunamis have struck the area in the past fifty years. The national park visitor center in Crescent City displays information about the Crescent City tsunamis.

The U.S. National Oceanic and Atmospheric Administration operates the West Coast and Alaska Tsunami Warning Center. Tsunamis generated off the coasts of Japan or Alaska take several hours to reach the California coast, which is usually ample time to warn residents to move away from shore and get to higher ground. It is important to remain away from

Tsunami hazard zone near Crescent City

the shoreline and low-lying areas until an official "all clear" is issued, which may be many hours later.

For tsunamis triggered by large earthquakes just offshore, there may not be sufficient time for adequate warning. The Cascadia Subduction Zone, where the Juan de Fuca and Gorda Plates are sliding beneath the North American Plate, has the potential to produce earthquakes with a very large vertical displacement along the northern California, Oregon, and Washington coasts. A tsunami could occur within minutes, so the earthquake itself is the warning that says, "Get to higher ground. Now!" Unusual beach conditions, such as the ocean receding rapidly away from the shoreline, may also signal an oncoming tsunami. The natural inclination of many people is to rush out to examine the sea stars, fish, crabs, and other marine life exposed on the newly revealed seafloor, but that impulse can kill.

8. PATRICK'S POINT STATE PARK
Franciscan Mélange and Younger Rocks

Patrick's Point State Park, located 25 miles north of Eureka, is a good place to see Franciscan mélange, a mixture of Franciscan Complex rocks so jumbled and convoluted by the great tectonic forces at work near the plate margins that the original deposition patterns were lost. The rocks were scraped off the ancient Farallon Plate as it was subducted beneath the North American Plate. At Patrick's Point, the Franciscan mélange includes outcrops of chert, greenstone, and blueschist scattered about within a shale matrix that is, in turn, mixed in with graywacke sandstone deposited by turbidity currents.

The greenstone is metamorphic pillow basalt. Blueschist is a metamorphic rock that forms in subduction zones when the original rock is subjected to high pressure but relatively low temperatures. The white veins running through the Franciscan rocks at Patrick's Point State Park are quartz and calcite. You can tell the difference between these two light-colored minerals because calcite is much softer than quartz.

Greenstone is more resistant to erosion than the surrounding graywacke sandstone, so it forms prominent sea stacks—the eroded remnants of headlands—both onshore and offshore. Wedding Rock is a partially detached sea stack, while Ceremonial and Lookout Rocks are residual sea stacks, formed when sea level was much higher and now stranded inland.

Patrick's Point State Park also features sedimentary layers much younger than the Franciscan rocks. Best exposed in the cliff behind Agate Beach, three distinct sedimentary units record a rising and falling sea level during the Pleistocene Ice Ages, from about 1.8 million to 11,500 years ago. A cooler climate increased the size of the polar ice caps so extensively that much more of Earth's water was locked up in ice, lowering sea level by several hundred feet. Crossbedded layers of sand indicate coastal sand dunes, formed during a period

Agate Beach, below cliffs of Pleistocene sedimentary rocks at Patrick's Point State Park

Wedding Rock, a sea stack of greenstone at Patrick's Point State Park

of lower sea level. During the interglacial periods, when sea level rose, mud was deposited in quiet lagoons, interspersed with cobbly storm deposits.

16

9. CACHE CREEK NATURAL AREA
The Great Valley Sequence

Home to bald eagles and tule elk, Cache Creek Natural Area is a 75,000-acre oak-studded park within easy reach of Sacramento and the Bay Area. Cache Creek flows east through progressively younger rocks of the Great Valley Sequence, layers of sandstone and shale deposited in a small ocean basin, known as a forearc basin, east of the subducting Farallon Plate. A forearc basin often forms between the accretionary wedge and the volcanic arc of a subduction zone. More resistant, buff-colored sandstone beds are interbedded with grayish black shale layers that are weak and easily eroded. The sediments built up during millions of years in Jurassic and Cretaceous time, slowly becoming solid rock as they were buried by other sediments. Tectonic forces at work near the boundary between the Pacific and North American Plates eventually uplifted and tilted the rock layers, now visible along Cache Creek.

The Great Valley Sequence within Cache Creek Natural Area is a series of marine sedimentary rocks deposited by turbidity currents, or underwater landslides. As the fast-moving current slows, gravel and sand particles settle out first, followed by the smaller silt and clay particles. Each current deposits a layer, known as a fining-up bed, that has coarse sediments at the base and finer sediments near the top. Eventually, another turbidity current deposits another fining-up bed. Over time, this process can create an impressive stack of fining-up beds, as seen along Cache Creek.

Steeply dipping shale of the Great Valley Sequence along Cache Creek at Cache Creek Natural Area

Sandstone of the Great Valley Sequence

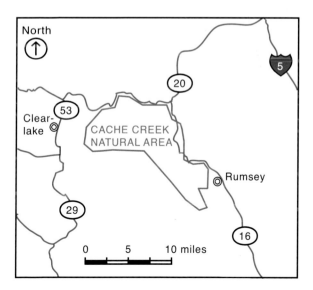

Crossed burrows (lower right corner). Camera lens cap for scale.

German Rancho Formation at Stump Beach

10. SALT POINT STATE PARK
Trace Fossils

Salt Point State Park, located approximately 30 miles north of Bodega Bay on California 1, has several scenic spots, including Horseshoe Cove, Fisk Mill Cove, and Gerstle Cove, but Stump Beach is the place to see geology. The beach is in a semiprotected cove at the mouth of Miller Creek. The tilted sandstone and mudstone layers surrounding Stump Beach are the German Rancho Formation, named for Rancho German, one of the largest 1840s-era land grant properties on the central Sonoma coast. The German Rancho marine sedimentary rocks lie on the Pacific Plate, on the west side of the San Andreas Fault. Inland, on the east side of the fault, Franciscan Complex rocks dominate the landscape. The German Rancho

Formation originated some 57 million years ago, far south of its current location, and was transported 200 miles north during the past 20 million years by plate tectonic movement along the San Andreas Fault.

You'll find an extensive assemblage of trace fossils embedded in the sandstone and mudstone layers that surround Stump Beach. Trace fossils are evidence of animal activity, rather than fossilized shells or hard body parts of the animals. Trace fossils typically include burrows, animal tracks, and coprolites (fossilized feces). Worms and other soft-bodied organisms typically don't fossilize, but the burrows they leave behind do, and that's what you'll see in the rocks at Stump Beach today. Look for short, 1-inch-long channels that cross between layers of rock, often a short sand channel in a mudstone layer. A burrowing organism, such as a worm, clam, or crab, lived in the mud, and while the burrow was still open, another layer of sediment, such as sand, covered and filled it. In addition to seeing cross sections of the burrows along their length, you can also find cross sections of their width on the top surfaces of rock layers. The latter appear as dots of different-colored sediment, such as sand spots in a mudstone layer.

The ends of burrows on a bedding surface at Stump Beach. Key for scale.

Stump Beach at Salt Point State Park

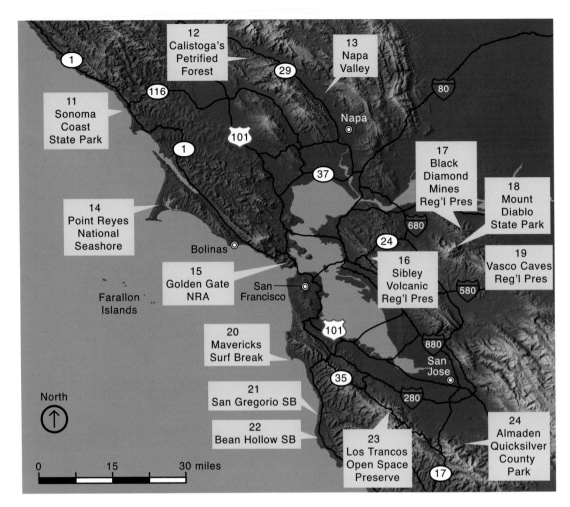

1 • 11 Sonoma Coast State Park • 116 • 12 Calistoga's Petrified Forest • 29 • 13 Napa Valley • 80 • 101 • Napa • 1 • 37 • 17 Black Diamond Mines Reg'l Pres • 18 Mount Diablo State Park • 14 Point Reyes National Seashore • 680 • 24 • 16 Sibley Volcanic Reg'l Pres • 19 Vasco Caves Reg'l Pres • Bolinas • 15 Golden Gate NRA • San Francisco • 580 • Farallon Islands • 20 Mavericks Surf Break • 101 • 880 • San Jose • 21 San Gregorio SB • 35 • 280 • 22 Bean Hollow SB • 23 Los Trancos Open Space Preserve • 24 Almaden Quicksilver County Park • 17

North

0   15   30 miles

SAN FRANCISCO BAY AREA

The geology of the San Francisco Bay Area is roughly defined by a series of three parallel north-south rock units: Salinian Block granites on the west side of the San Andreas Fault, which underlie San Francisco Peninsula and Point Reyes, Franciscan Complex rocks through the central Bay Area, and Great Valley sedimentary rocks to the east of the East Bay Hills. All these units came into play over a period of tens of millions of years of tectonic activity, first through subduction of the Farallon Plate beneath the North American Plate, and then due to horizontal movement along the San Andreas Fault system as the Pacific Plate slowly moved northwest relative to the North American Plate. Movement along the San Andreas and related faults continues to shape the Bay Area today.

11. SONOMA COAST STATE PARK
Sea Stacks

Sonoma Coast State Park, which stretches more than 15 miles from Bodega Head to north of Jenner, encompasses a wealth of coastal landforms, including sea stacks, arches, coastal sand dunes, and marine terraces. Goat Rock Beach, at the mouth of the Russian River, may look inviting, but be wary: its cold water, treacherous rip currents, and hidden drop-offs make swimming inadvisable. Instead, enjoy the view of Goat Rock, a partially detached sea stack, made of resistant rock that remains after the surrounding rock has eroded away. The grayish graywacke making up Goat Rock is a sandstone deposited by a turbidity current.

Arch Rock, one of many arches along the California coast, is visible offshore from the Blind Beach trailhead for the Kortum Trail. Arches form when ocean waves erode a slot through a sea stack. The top of the arch, beyond the reach of ocean waves, erodes more slowly but will eventually collapse into the sea. Just south of Blind Beach, the Kortum Trail rises to its highest elevation as it crosses a saddle on the north side of 377-foot-high Peaked Hill. From the saddle, the trail drops to a nearly flat marine terrace, a wave-cut platform now high and dry. Two ancient sea stacks rise, shiplike, from the grass-covered marine terrace. Locally called Sunset Rocks, these sea stacks are outcrops of blueschist and chert that were resistant to the wave action that cut the marine terrace when sea level was higher relative to the land.

Sea stacks on the Sonoma Coast

Sea stacks on a marine terrace along the Kortum Trail in Sonoma Coast State Park

View to the south along the Sonoma Coast, with Arch Rock offshore

12. CALISTOGA'S PETRIFIED FOREST
Petrified Wood

Calistoga's Petrified Forest is worth a short detour from wine excursions in the Napa Valley. Petrified wood is rare, and petrified forests rarer still, because they only form under unique geologic conditions. Here, the precipitating event was a volcanic eruption near Mount Saint Helena, north of Calistoga, some 3.2 million years ago. The explosive eruption blew down an entire forest of redwoods and pine trees, and successive eruptions and occasional mudflows completely buried the forest. Because the trees were entombed in a thick layer of high-silica rhyolite ash that prevented oxygen from reaching them, there was virtually no decomposition of the wood by insects or fungi. Later still, perhaps in conjunction with a rising water table, the buried trees were soaked in a silica-rich stew from the chemical weathering of the rhyolite ash. Over a period of thousands of years, the silica solution replaced each individual wood cell. The resulting silica rock, a type of quartz, is a finely detailed stone replica of the original wood, with the bark and individual tree rings completely preserved. See site 16, Sibley Volcanic Regional Preserve, for a discussion of why there was volcanic activity here in the last 5 million years.

Credit for developing the petrified forest into a tourist attraction goes to Ollie Bockee, who purchased the land in 1914, when only two petrified trees were visible. Over the next three decades, she supervised the excavation of a dozen more petrified trees and also sent a 3-ton log to New York City and donated another large specimen to the 1915 Pan-American Exposition in San Francisco.

The Giant, a large petrified log at Calistoga's Petrified Forest

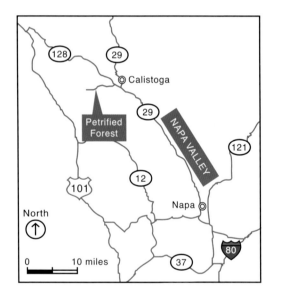

Close-up view of petrified wood

22

Napa Valley vineyard

13. NAPA VALLEY
Terroir of Wine

"For picturesque beauty and general salubrity of climate, it would not be easy to decide which of the valleys leading out from the Bay of San Francisco is entitled to pre-eminence; taken together, they may well claim to be considered as one of the most attractive portions of our country." So wrote Josiah Whitney in his 1865 report detailing the first comprehensive geological survey of the state. One of the picturesque valleys he described is Napa Valley, home to California's wine industry. The unique blend of climate, aspect, and rocky soil, combined with high-quality grape stock and the vintner's skill, come together to produce some of the world's finest wines.

Napa County's famous soil is derived from a unique blend of metamorphic, sedimentary, and igneous rocks. Wine professionals use the French term *terroir* to describe how the flavors of a wine reflect the unique qualities of the earth in the place where the grapes are grown. A wine's terroir develops from many qualities beyond just soil, including slope, temperature, precipitation, wind patterns, and amount of sunshine. Napa's soil is derived from a mix of Franciscan Complex rocks, Great Valley sedimentary rocks, and Sonoma Volcanics. The Franciscan Complex, which dominates the Coast Ranges, is the product of subduction of the Farallon Plate beneath the North American Plate.

The Great Valley Sequence consists of layers of marine sandstone and shale deposited in a forearc ocean basin east of the subducting Farallon Plate. Weathering of Napa Valley rocks, especially the volcanic rocks and the Franciscan Complex serpentinite, produces poor-quality soil. Serpentinite contains high concentrations of nickel and chromium, which are toxic to most plants, and is also relatively low in essential nutrients such as calcium and potassium. Oddly though, grape vines flourish here, reaching their roots deep into the soil to extract the limited nutrients available. In fact, this dynamic is common in viticulture; many of the world's best wines come from grape vines that struggle to survive.

23

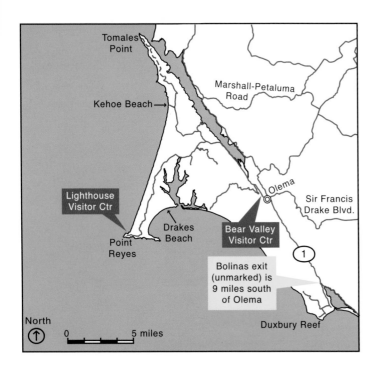

Granitic rock along the Tomales Point coastline

14. POINT REYES NATIONAL SEASHORE
The San Andreas Fault and the Rocks It Brought with It

In his 1865 publication documenting four years of fieldwork, California state geologist Josiah Whitney wrote of Point Reyes, "The principal ridge is on the western side, and is separated from the ridges east by a nearly straight valley, the northern portion of which, for about 15 miles, is occupied by Tomales Bay, the remainder by the swamps at the head of the bay and the valley of Arroyo Olemus Loke, terminating on the south in Baulines Bay, thus forming a well-marked and continuous depression through the entire distance."

Little did Josiah know that the "well-marked and continuous depression" he described was the San Andreas Fault Zone, the boundary between the Pacific Plate and the North American Plate. Three faults merge in Bolinas Lagoon: the San Gregorio, San Andreas, and Golden Gate Faults. The Point Reyes Peninsula moved north from the Big Sur and Salinas area along the San Gregorio Fault, which is a spur of the San Andreas.

Long before it was a national seashore, Point Reyes was shaken hard by the 1906 San Francisco earthquake. A farm fence was offset nearly 20 feet, and a train was toppled from the tracks. The Point Reyes Earthquake Trail, a half-mile loop near the Bear Valley Visitor Center, documents ground movement of the 1906 earthquake, along with regional Bay Area geology.

The core of Point Reyes consists of 82-million-year-old granitic rocks, which are overlain by progressively younger layers of sedimentary rock. The layers were deposited in the ocean offshore of Point Reyes while the peninsula was migrating north to its current position. We know that the Purisima Formation is the youngest of the Tertiary-age sedimentary rocks at Point Reyes because it overlies the Santa Cruz Mudstone (exposed at Duxbury Reef), the Monterey Formation and Laird Sandstone (exposed at Kehoe Beach), and the Point Reyes Conglomerate (exposed at the lighthouse).

Two of the best places to see the granitic basement rocks are at Pierce Point Ranch and along the Tomales Point Trail, which extends through the Tule Elk Reserve. The granitic rocks of Point Reyes are a complicated mix of intrusive igneous types, including granite, granodiorite, quartz diorite, and tonalite.

The Monterey Formation and Laird Sandstone overlie the granite on the west side of Inverness Ridge and are best exposed at Kehoe Beach. The Monterey Formation, which consists of layers of pale, fine-grained rocks such as shale and siltstone, is exposed in the cliffs at the west end of the Kehoe Beach Trail. To the north along Kehoe Beach, the thin layers of the Monterey Formation grade into thicker (and older) layers of Laird Sandstone. A few hundred feet farther north, the Laird Sandstone abuts the granitic basement rocks of Point Reyes. A reverse fault, formed by compressive forces, separates the granite from the Laird Sandstone. The granitic rocks here are crisscrossed by multiple light-colored feldspar dikes, which formed when magma intruded the still-cooling fractured granitic mass.

The 302-step descent to the Point Reyes Lighthouse, on the southwestern tip of the peninsula, is one of the only places in the park to see outcrops of the Point Reyes Conglomerate. This sedimentary rock unit is made up of well-rounded cobbles

Monterey Formation at Kehoe Beach

A reverse fault separating granitic basement rock (left) and Laird Sandstone (right) at Kehoe Beach

Point Reyes Conglomerate on the trail to the Point Reyes Lighthouse

in a sandy matrix and interbedded with layers of coarse sandstone. The conglomerate and sandstone originated from material sloughed off land and deposited in a submarine fan at the mouth of a deep sea canyon. A submarine fan is similar in shape to the alluvial fans common to high-relief deserts such as Death Valley, but the material in a submarine fan is better sorted because of being deposited in water. The conglomerate is essentially identical to the Carmelo Formation exposed near Point Lobos south of Monterey. In fact, both rocks may have been deposited in the same submarine canyon but now lie separated by more than 100 miles because of offset along the San Gregorio and San Andreas Faults.

Drakes Beach, on the protected south side of the Point Reyes Peninsula, is named for Sir Francis Drake, an English privateer who careened his ship the *Golden Hind* in the bay's shallow waters on June 17, 1579. In the days before dry docks were readily available, careening a ship was a method to expose the keel for repairs and maintenance. A captain would beach his ship in shallow water, then load provisions (or, in Drake's case, plundered gold) on one side of the ship to weight it down and cause the vessel to roll toward port or starboard. Using ropes attached to the mast, the ship's crew would pull the ship over even farther, exposing the keel

Chunk of the Purisima Formation at Drakes Beach

Cliff of the Purisima Formation at Drakes Beach

so they could remove barnacles, repair holes, and caulk leaks in the hull.

To Drake and his crew, the 200-foot-high sedimentary cliffs were reminiscent of the white cliffs of Dover, England. Those 300-foot-high white cliffs are chalk, formed from billions of coccoliths, plates that made up the calcium carbonate shells of single-celled algae. However, the cliffs at Drake's Beach are quite different in origin, being buff to yellow layers of mudstone, siltstone, and sandstone of the Purisima Formation. The Drakes Beach cliffs, like all cliffs at Point Reyes, are best admired from a distance, as rockfalls are common.

After two months of repairs, Captain Drake refloated the *Golden Hind* and continued westward across the Pacific Ocean and back to England, where he became Sir Francis Drake after Queen Elizabeth knighted him in 1581.

Duxbury Reef, adjacent to the well-hidden town of Bolinas, is the southernmost extremity of the Point Reyes Peninsula. The reef, protected within the Gulf of the Farallones National Marine Sanctuary, is made up of steeply tilted beds of Santa Cruz Mudstone, which was deposited from about 11 to 5 million years ago. Softer mudstone layers eroded faster than harder layers, creating the rough topography, which provides a haven for intertidal wildlife, including sea stars, sea anemones, hermit crabs, mussels, sea urchins, and small fish. To reach Duxbury Reef, take the (unmarked) Bolinas exit from California 1, located 9 miles south of Olema or about 5 miles north of Stinson Beach. From Olema-Bolinas Road, turn right on Mesa Road, left on Overlook, then right on Elm Street, and park in the lot at Agate Beach County Park.

Sea anemones in a tide pool at Duxbury Reef

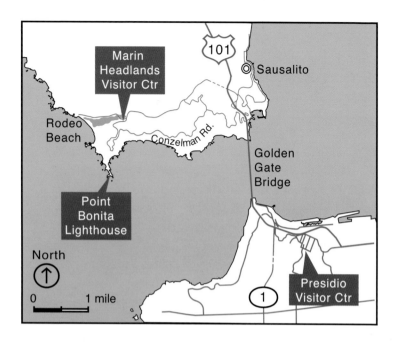

15. GOLDEN GATE NATIONAL RECREATION AREA
Radiolarian Chert and Pillow Basalt

The southern tip of Marin County, including the Marin Headlands unit of Golden Gate National Recreation Area, is the best place to get to know radiolarian chert of the Franciscan Complex. This distinctive, reddish brown, layered and tightly folded rock formation makes up 50 percent of the headlands. Rodeo Beach, Tennessee Valley, Hawk Hill, McCullough Road, Bunker Road, and Conzelman Road all have extensive outcrops of radiolarian chert. Radiolaria are microscopic marine organisms (zooplankton) that have silica skeletons. Over millions of years, a constant rain of dead zooplankton built up on the seafloor. Eventually, these radiolarian deposits were

Radiolarian chert along Conzelman Road in the Marin Headlands

compacted and hardened to form chert, a silica-rich sedimentary rock. Transported eastward on the Farallon Plate, the radiolarian chert (as well as other rocks of the Franciscan Complex) was accreted onto the North American Plate as the Farallon Plate was subducted.

Radiolarian chert is more resistant to erosion than other Franciscan rocks such as serpentinite, pillow basalt, and graywacke. Its durability makes it a common outcrop on peaks throughout San Francisco, including Mount Davidson, Twin Peaks, Golden Gate Heights Park, and Corona Heights. Chocolate brown is the most common color, but green and black varieties are also present in the Marin Headlands and elsewhere in the Bay Area. Reddish radiolarian chert gives

Red Rock, a small island visible just south of the Richmond end of the Richmond–San Rafael Bridge, its name. The chert's distinctive, tightly folded, thin layers make it easy to recognize amidst the Bay Area's chaotic landscape.

Point Bonita

The half-mile trail to Point Bonita in the Marin Headlands crosses five bridges before reaching the lighthouse. The final bridge to the lighthouse sways alarmingly over a narrow ridge of pillow basalt that's part of the Franciscan Complex. Pillow basalt forms when hot lava erupts underwater and is instantly quenched. New hot lava continues to erupt, only to be rapidly chilled, so pillow basalt features many bulbous

Point Bonita Lighthouse resting precariously on pillow basalt of the Franciscan Complex

Point Bonita

Pillow basalt outcrop below the Point Bonita Lighthouse

shapes that resemble a bunch of pillows. The pillow basalt found at Point Bonita erupted at a mid-ocean ridge over 180 million years ago. Tectonic movement carried the pillow basalt eastward atop the Farallon Plate until it collided with the North American Plate. Although most of the oceanic plate was subducted, small fragments, including the Marin Headlands, were scraped off and piled onto the continent. These plate fragments, called accretionary wedges, form the rocks of today's Coast Ranges.

In addition to the spectacular view from Point Bonita's promontory, the lighthouse contains a fascinating record of more than four hundred shipwrecks in and near the Golden Gate.

16. SIBLEY VOLCANIC REGIONAL PRESERVE
Young Volcanics in the Coast Range

Tucked in the East Bay Hills between Tilden Regional Park to the north and Redwood Regional Park to the south, Sibley Volcanic Regional Preserve includes some of the Bay Area's best volcanic features. Sibley's volcanic center is the 1,763-foot-high hill called Round Top, the focal point of eruptive activity some 10 million years ago.

The geologically recent volcanic activity here and elsewhere in the Coast Ranges is related to the Mendocino Triple Junction, which is where three tectonic plates meet just off the coast of Mendocino. It is also the northern end of the San Andreas Fault. As the plate boundary at the western edge of North America changed over the last 20 million years from a subduction zone to the San Andreas Fault, a transform boundary, the location of the triple junction migrated approximately 450 miles north from the central coast to Mendocino, traveling at a rate of only 1 or 2 inches per year.

Triple junctions are tectonically active, as plate movement produces numerous earthquakes and, frequently, volcanoes. This triple junction is responsible for the volcanic rock in the East Bay Hills and in the Sonoma and Clear Lake areas.

Before Sibley Volcanic Regional Preserve was a park, Kaiser Sand and Gravel quarried basalt here for road construction. The two quarries have opened a window to the subsurface, illuminating the intricate network of basalt layers within the Round Top volcano system. During the past 10 million years, movement along the Hayward Fault, which runs just east of Sibley Volcanic Regional Preserve, tilted the entire Round Top volcano on its side, upending the basalt layers. Several rock outcrops within the park show good examples of both massive and vesicular basalt. Vesicles, or cavities, form when gas bubbles are trapped in cooling lava.

Steeply tilted volcanic layers at Sibley Volcanic Regional Preserve

31

17. BLACK DIAMOND MINES REGIONAL PRESERVE
California Coal

To downhill skiers, *black diamond* refers to a challenging ski run. To nineteenth-century miners, however, *black diamonds* meant coal. During the late nineteenth century, the Black Diamond Coal Mine was California's largest, with nearly 4 million tons of coal produced over forty years. The two main coal seams, the Clark Vein and the Black Diamond Vein, were layers within the Domengine Formation, a predominantly marine sandstone unit nearly 450 feet thick. After the coal supply was exhausted, the high-quality quartz sand of the Domengine was mined to provide raw material for glassmaking.

Although laterally extensive, the coal beds were only a few feet thick and consisted primarily of lignite, a relatively poor-quality coal. However, it was the most significant coal in the Bay Area in the nineteenth century. Coal forms when plants die in swampy, humid environments and are submerged. The carbon sequestered in the plant material is preserved rather than being lost to the atmosphere through decay and oxidation. With time, the dead submerged plants form peat, a precursor of coal. If layers of sediment bury the peat, the pressure of compaction eventually forms coal of varying quality, ranging from lignite to subbituminous, bituminous, and, finally, anthracite, the highest-value coal.

In association with the regional uplift of Mount Diablo, the Domengine Formation tilts, or dips, at about 20 to 30 degrees to the north. The dip angle made it economically impractical to excavate the coal by open-pit mining methods, so tunnels were dug deep underground. Underground mining was physically demanding and dangerous, exposing miners to the risks of tunnel ceiling collapse, asphyxiation due to poor air quality, and explosions of ever-present methane gas and coal dust. Even if they survived these dangers, black lung disease afflicted many miners. In the late nineteenth century, young children were employed as "nobbers" in the mine, responsible for pushing the coal along narrow tunnels to waiting ore carts. Today, guided underground walking tours travel through the Domengine sandstone to explore the former Hazel-Atlas mine.

A coal seam a few inches thick, with parts of the tunnel support system showing in the wood at the top of the photo and the concrete diagonal piece at lower right

A tunnel carved in the Domengine Formation inside the former Hazel-Atlas mine

Mount Diablo from Walnut Creek

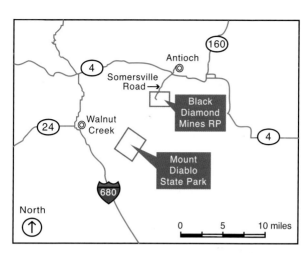

18. MOUNT DIABLO STATE PARK
Trail Through Time

At 3,849 feet, Mount Diablo, or "Devil Mountain," dominates the horizon of the East Bay and beyond. The peak is such a prominent landmark that it served as an anchor point for early California maps. Before the advent of Universal Transverse Mercator coordinates, parcel maps used a township and range coordinate system, which relied on prominent landmarks to serve as control points for surveys. Mount Diablo was one such control point, and even today, it's not unusual to find old parcel maps referring to the Mount Diablo Baseline.

Mount Diablo isn't the highest peak in the Bay Area. San Jose's Mount Hamilton is 500 feet higher, but it's tucked in among other peaks, so it isn't as prominent as Mount Diablo, which stands alone. Mount Diablo's height is the culmination of millions of years of seismic activity along the network of faults that surround and transect it, including the Concord, Marsh Creek, and Kirker Faults. Mount Diablo was never a volcano, which is a common misperception, although ocean floor basalts do occur there, the product of accretion of rocks of the Farallon Plate during its subduction.

The two main summits and central part of Mount Diablo consist of graywacke, altered pillow basalt (greenstone), radiolarian chert, and some minor shale and blueschist of the Franciscan Complex. The margins of Mount Diablo, however, are more complicated, particularly on the north side, which is dominated by Mount Diablo ophiolite and cut by dozens of small faults. An ophiolite is a specific sequence of very dense rocks from the oceanic crust and upper mantle.

The Trail Through Time, a 6-mile hiking route with interpretive signs, extends from Blackhawk Road to the summit of Mount Diablo, a 2,900-foot elevation gain. The trail travels back through time, passing first through 9-million-year-old river deposits, then through

Mortars in Domengine sandstone, used by Native Americans of the Bay Miwok Tribe for grinding acorns

15-million-year-old nearshore marine sedimentary rocks to even older deepwater sedimentary rocks, and then, finally, to rocks of the Franciscan Complex, as much as 190 million years old, on the summit.

19. VASCO CAVES REGIONAL PRESERVE
Concretions in Sandstone

Vasco Caves Regional Preserve is only accessible through guided tours organized by the East Bay Regional Park District. Located east of Mount Diablo, Vasco is a fragile ecosystem with unique geology. The predominant rock type is weakly cemented, easily eroded sandstone—so easily eroded, in fact, that water and wind have produced the "caves" scattered throughout the park, which are actually just hollows in the sandstone. Some of the hollows are deep enough to have provided temporary shelter for Native Americans who lived in the region for perhaps 10,000 years.

The sandstone encloses hundreds of large concretions, round balls of hard rock. Concretions can form in sedimentary rocks due to physical, chemical, or biological changes that occur as the sediments pile up. Concretions commonly form around an organic center, such as a leaf or bone fragment. Minerals precipitate preferentially around the nucleus, forming a denser, ball-shaped rock that is more resistant to erosion than the sedimentary rock. As the surrounding soft sandstone erodes away, the concretions remain, until finally there's no supporting rock left and they roll downhill. You may see groups of concretions at the base of an eroding sandstone cliff. Although concretions can range from the size of grapes to the size of beach balls or larger, some of those at Vasco Caves Regional Preserve are quite large, with diameters exceeding 3 feet.

Sandstone outcrops at Vasco Caves Regional Preserve

A concretion eroding from a sandstone cliff at Vasco Caves Regional Preserve

34

20. MAVERICKS SURF BREAK
Seafloor Topography

Surfing is all about geology. The nearshore rock structure, combined with swell, tide, and wind conditions, create the big waves found at Mavericks Surf Break. Although the largest waves occur here for only a few days each year, Mavericks is one of the world's best big-wave surf breaks, and a surfing contest is held here each year. Because contest-height waves can only be predicted about twenty-four hours in advance, the two dozen invited surfers are on call during the big-wave season and have twenty-four hours to arrive at the beach. The contest, which is best viewed via the internet because the waves break a half mile offshore, may include wave faces over 40 feet tall.

Recent mapping of the seafloor topography here has revealed the secret of Mavericks. A series of tightly folded sedimentary rocks have eroded in such a way that an area of deep water quickly shallows at a fin-shaped reef. Waves coming from the west tend to wrap around the reef on the seafloor, converging to form the massive waves that define Mavericks.

The waves only break when the swell is big enough, typically more than 15 feet high. Smaller swells simply roll over the reef, breaking closer to shore. The reef, which surfers call the Boneyard due to the rough seafloor here, is only about 18 feet deep. Movement along the San Gregorio Fault, which cuts through Pillar Point, likely folded the rocks here.

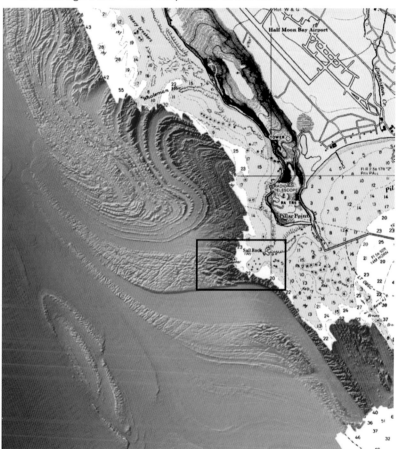

Bathymetry (underwater topography) of Mavericks. Color ranges from red (shallow) to blue (deep). The white area is water that is too shallow to survey due to limited boat access. The black box shows the surfing area. The beige area is land. —Image courtesy of the National Oceanic and Atmospheric Administration

Surfers on a Mavericks wave. —Photo by Seth Migdail

35

21. SAN GREGORIO STATE BEACH
Sea Caves and Trace Fossils

San Gregorio State Beach has several fine sea caves in the Purisima Formation (deposited 7 to 2.6 million years ago) that are accessible at low tide. Sea caves form when the pounding of ocean waves erodes and washes away weaker rock that has an overlying zone of more resistant rock. The resistant rock at San Gregorio is a layer of buff-colored sandstone. The weaker rock is a grayish green layer of weaker sandstone. Sea caves may also form along faults. The ground-up material in the fault zone is often weaker than the rocks that bound it, making it more susceptible to erosion.

In addition to sea caves, San Gregorio State Beach has excellent examples of trace fossils, which preserve geologic evidence of animal activity. At San Gregorio, the trace fossils are burrows from marine organisms, such as crabs or worms, that lived approximately 5.3 to 2.6 million years ago, during Pliocene time. The burrows at San Gregorio are most visible at the interface between the buff sandstone and the grayish green sandstone. Many of the burrows are finger-sized or larger. Some of the short, disconnected burrows connect to the overlying buff sandstone layer, though the connection is not obvious in the cliff face because the burrows are at an angle.

Sea cave at San Gregorio State Beach

22. BEAN HOLLOW STATE BEACH
Tafoni and Graded Bedding

Bean Hollow State Beach on the San Mateo coast is notable for tafoni and graded bedding in the Pigeon Point Formation, which is a turbidity current deposit (turbidite). Tafoni (singular: tafone) are pits and hollows in the rock surface thought to be caused by differential weathering and, possibly, differential cementation. Rain, which is naturally acidic, may dissolve the sandstone's calcium carbonate cement, the glue that holds its individual sand grains together. The calcium carbonate migrates to the surface of the rock, forming a hard crust, but the interior of the rock is left relatively weak by the loss of calcium carbonate. When a small part of the cemented surface rock is weathered away, the interior weathers more quickly, forming a hole.

Tafoni are frequently found in coastal areas and saline-rich desert environments, where salt contributes to the weathering, perhaps by chemical interactions with the rock matrix or by physical expansion of salt crystals during the crystallization process. Microclimates within the developing pit may enhance tafoni weathering. Because air entering a shaded tafone condenses, moisture settles on the interior wall.

Sedimentary layers that show a gradation in particle sizes are called graded beds. When a turbidity current, or underwater landslide, begins to slow, gravity sorts the material as it settles deep undersea. Heavier gravel and coarse sand particles settle out first, followed by successively smaller sand, silt, and clay particles. At Bean Hollow State Beach, beds of the Pigeon Point Formation are tilted almost upright, so you can see the eroded edges of the graded bedding as you scramble about the rocks.

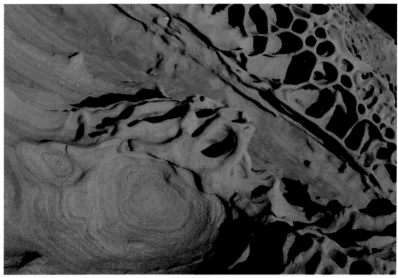

Tafoni weathering at Bean Hollow State Beach

Graded bedding at Bean Hollow State Beach

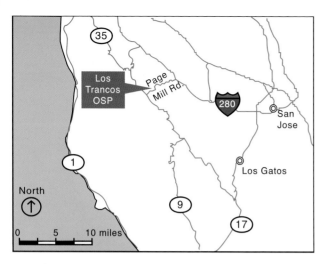

Sag pond formed in a depression along the San Andreas Fault at Los Trancos Open Space Preserve

23. LOS TRANCOS OPEN SPACE PRESERVE
The 1906 Earthquake

One of the best places to see the effects of the massive 1906 San Francisco earthquake on the San Andreas Fault is in Los Trancos Open Space Preserve, which is part of the Midpeninsula Regional Open Space District. Nine stops along the 1.5-mile loop of the San Andreas Fault Trail allow visitors an up-close view of features along the fault. Even with erosion and vegetation growth, the century-old scars are still visible. Movement along the fault created the small pond (dry for much of the year) next to the parking lot. This type of feature, called a sag pond, is common throughout the Bay Area. San Andreas Lake, west of Millbrae, is one of the largest sag ponds on the San Francisco Peninsula. Although expanded by a dam, San Andreas Lake originated as a topographic depression along the fault boundary.

From stop 2, the trail descends downhill to the main 1906 rupture. The cracks in the ground have long since filled in, but the combined effect of multiple earthquakes over many millennia has left a roadlike platform that runs along the slope of the hillside.

Stop 4 is at a short section of wooden fence offset 3 feet where it crosses the San Andreas Fault. Although the offset

An oak, toppled by the 1906 earthquake, continuing to grow at Los Trancos Open Space Preserve

fence is a reconstruction, it provides a graphic example of the power of earthquakes. You'll need to look carefully at stop 7 to see the strangest feature on the trail: Two oaks at this location were shaken, dislodged, and tipped over to nearly horizontal during the 1906 quake. However, the earthquake didn't destroy their root structures, so the newly vertical tree limbs grew into multiple trunks, forming two very odd-looking trees.

24. ALMADEN QUICKSILVER COUNTY PARK
Mercury Mine

New Almaden, an active mercury mine for more than a century, started operating at an auspicious time in California's history—just two years before gold was discovered in the state. New Almaden was perfectly positioned to provide much-needed mercury to the Sierra goldfields. Because mercury, or "quicksilver," combines with gold, it is used to separate gold from other rock. When the gold-mercury mixture is heated, the mercury evaporates, leaving gold.

The mercury, which occurs in cinnabar ore, was deposited by hydrothermal fluid in fracture zones in rocks of the Franciscan Complex. Rarer even than gold, cinnabar exists in economically viable concentrations at only a few locations worldwide, including in the California Coast Ranges. At New Almaden, the richest cinnabar ore contained as much as 60 percent mercury by weight. Processing cinnabar is a relatively simple process. Raw ore is crushed in a mill and then roasted to vaporize the mercury. The mercury vapor is then cooled until it condenses. This millennia-old mercury reduction process was improved at New Almaden, and by 1880, New Almaden's mercury processing technique was among the best in the world.

Any visit to Almaden Quicksilver County Park should start at Casa Grande, the park's visitor center and museum on Almaden Road. One of the best trails in the park in

terms of mining-related features is the Wood Road/Castillero/Mine Hill loop, which passes by the rotary furnace (the main mercury processing facility), as well as the San Cristobal mine entrance. You can explore about 150 feet of the San Cristobal Tunnel, after which it is blocked by a bat-friendly gate.

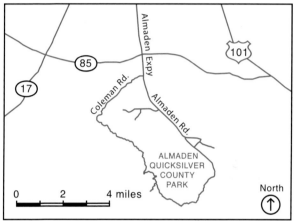

Mercury flasks at Almaden Quicksilver County Park. A standard flask contains 76 pounds of mercury.

Former mercury processing facility at Almaden Quicksilver County Park

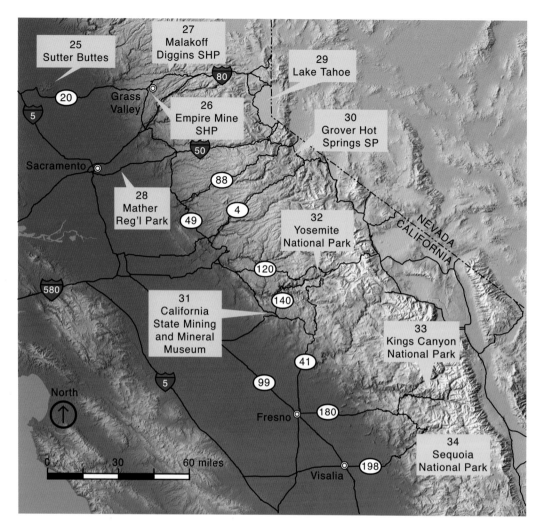

25 Sutter Buttes

27 Malakoff Diggins SHP

29 Lake Tahoe

26 Empire Mine SHP

30 Grover Hot Springs SP

28 Mather Reg'l Park

32 Yosemite National Park

31 California State Mining and Mineral Museum

33 Kings Canyon National Park

34 Sequoia National Park

Grass Valley

Sacramento

NEVADA
CALIFORNIA

Fresno

Visalia

North

0   30   60 miles

SIERRA NEVADA

The Sierra Nevada (a Spanish name meaning the "snowy range") runs north-south for more than 400 miles near the eastern boundary of California. This range is home to some of the state's most scenic places, including Yosemite, Sequoia, and Kings Canyon National Parks. Granitic rocks of the Sierra originated from subduction of the Farallon Plate beneath the North American Plate. Heat generated by the subduction zone melted the overlying crust, forming magma, or molten rock. Between about 210 and 80 million years ago, the magma cooled deep underground in a series of plutons, or distinct bodies of granitic igneous rock. Together, hundreds of plutons form the Sierra Nevada Batholith. Hot fluids circulating through the cooling plutons and adjacent rock deposited gold and other minerals. Over time, vertical movement of faults on the east side of the Sierra brought the granitic rocks aboveground, raising the range to the lofty heights seen today.

25. SUTTER BUTTES
A Young Volcanic Center

Located just a few miles west of Marysville, Sutter Buttes are peaks within a young volcano that erupted less than 2 million years ago. Early geologist Howell Williams envisioned the buttes as a castle emerging from the floor of the Sacramento Valley and gave the features the fanciful terms still in use today—castellated core, moat, and ramparts. The rocks of the castellated core, which form the rocky peaks visible for miles, are primarily rhyolite and andesite. The rhyolite at Sutter Buttes, which forms characteristic rounded hills, is light gray and fine-grained. The andesite rocks are darker, form high craggy peaks, and are quite rich in crystals.

The silica-rich rhyolite erupted first, emerging from vents around the edge of the future volcano, made of andesite, which has a lower silica content. Both the rhyolite and the andesite erupted through the existing sedimentary rock. The remnants of the weak, easily eroded sedimentary rock form the moat, which rings the castellated core. The ramparts, which circle the castellated core and the moat, consist of hot rocks and ash that were ejected from eruption vents in the castellated core, forming a broad apron of material around Sutter Buttes.

Long before California's system of levees and reservoirs was developed, winter rains and spring snowmelt frequently flooded the Sacramento Valley. At those times, travelers crossed through Sutter Buttes rather than circumnavigating the flooded ground. Today, most of Sutter Buttes is under private ownership and is used primarily for orchards and sheep and cattle ranching. The Middle Mountain Foundation, a regional land trust that serves to protect the unique cultural and natural resources of Sutter Buttes, has a cadre of volunteers who lead hiking trips into the area.

Rounded hill of rhyolite (left) and jagged peaks of andesite (right) at Sutter Buttes

Looking east toward Sutter Buttes

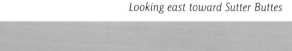

41

26. EMPIRE MINE STATE HISTORIC PARK
Hard Rock Gold Mine

Grass Valley's Empire Mine, which operated from 1850 to 1956, was one of the richest hard rock mines in California. During the mine's 106-year operating history, nearly 6 million ounces of gold were extracted from 367 miles of tunnels. The Empire is a classic Grass Valley District mine, and but one of many that operated in the late 1800s. In the Grass Valley District, gold was found in quartz veins cutting two different host rocks. The first rock type is the igneous rock granodiorite, which is slightly darker and more rich in plagioclase than granite. The quartz veins in the granodiorite generally dip (tilt) less than 35 degrees from horizontal. The second host rock is a mix of the metamorphic rocks serpentinite and amphibolite. Quartz veins in the metamorphic rock typically dip at much steeper angles, making them more difficult to mine. The ore in both units is exceptionally rich.

Miners from Cornwall, England, who had centuries of experience in hard rock copper and tin mining, provided the bulk of the labor force. They brought innovative mining methods to the Empire Mine, including the Cornish pump, used to remove water from the mine tunnels—a constant problem in mines that extend below the water table. The Cornish pump, capable of extracting more than 3,000 gallons per minute, enabled the miners to tunnel more than a mile below ground surface.

The park's visitor center features the former mine owner's elaborate scale model of the mine's entire 367-mile network of tunnels. Every mile was mapped three-dimensionally in a rainbow of color-coded wire, with warmer colors (red and orange) signifying the richest ore.

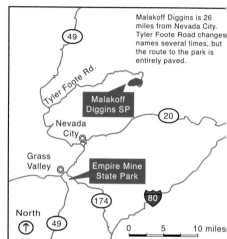

Malakoff Diggins is 26 miles from Nevada City. Tyler Foote Road changes names several times, but the route to the park is entirely paved.

Ore carts at Empire Mine State Historic Park

Headframe (the structure above a mine shaft that supports the hoist equipment) at Empire Mine State Historic Park

Hydraulic mine pit at Malakoff Diggins State Historic Park

A water cannon, called a monitor, pointed at a placer deposit at Malakoff Diggins State Historic Park

27. MALAKOFF DIGGINS STATE HISTORIC PARK
Hydraulic Mining of Placer Deposits

The earliest California gold miners, the forty-niners who arrived in the goldfields from 1848 to 1849, simply panned for gold, swishing water and gravel around in a pan to separate the gold from the gravel. However, they quickly developed better methods to tease out the gold, using sluice boxes, rockers, and Long Toms. Given the rapid influx of tens of thousands of miners to northern California, the supply of gold in the Sierra's active stream channels was largely exhausted within a few years. Miners soon realized, however, that far more gold was available in ancient streambeds—sand and gravel beds often hundreds of feet thick. Known as placer deposits when they contain valuable minerals, here they were enriched in gold due to millions of years of sifting by ancient streams. These deposits weren't necessarily near modern water sources, and water was needed to extract the gold.

Where there's money to be made, technology will find a way. Miners constructed miles of flumes, ditches, and canals to deliver water to the placer deposits. The entire water transportation network was fed by gravity, with the gradual drop in elevation providing the power needed to blast away whole hillsides of gold-bearing gravel, a technique called hydraulic mining. Water cannons, known as monitors, gave the system the 5,000-pounds-per-square-inch force needed to wash away millennia of alluvial deposits. The monitors, some of which were more than 15 feet long, could send a jet of water more than 400 feet. The sand and gravel slurry was directed to giant sluice boxes to recover the gold. Hydraulic mining, which proved to be a highly effective method of gold extraction, reached its peak in California in the late 1860s.

Hydraulic mining was also highly damaging to the environment. Entire hillsides were washed away in a matter of days, sending a muddy mixture of sand and gravel downslope to fields and farms in the Central Valley. In 1875, a flood buried Marysville under several feet of waste material, called slickens. The flatlanders filed lawsuits, resulting in an 1884 injunction written by judge Lorenzo Sawyer to limit the discharge of slickens. Although the Sawyer decision didn't ban hydraulic mining outright, it placed tight controls on the management of mine waste material and sounded the death knell for hydraulic mining in the Sierra Nevada.

43

28. MATHER REGIONAL PARK
Vernal Pools

The hummocky, undulating landscape of Mather Regional Park makes it one of the best places in California to see vernal pools, shallow depressions in the ground that fill up with water during winter rains, bloom with life for a few weeks in springtime, and then dry up for the rest of the year. Vernal pools form in a variety of environments; the secret to the formation of the Mather vernal pools is two hard soil layers that limit drainage.

Hardpan, a dense soil layer, occurs about 2 to 4 feet below the base of Mather's vernal pools. Silica in the hardpan has filled in pore spaces between individual sand grains, forming a tight seal that limits downward migration of water. Soils in the Mather area, including the Hedge, the Redding, and—California's official state soil—the San Joaquin, contain abundant silica.

The second type of hard soil layer responsible for vernal pools at Mather, called claypan, forms in humid environments as chemical, physical, and biological weathering breaks soil into smaller and smaller particles. The ultimate product, clay, settles at the base of the vernal pool. Combined with the deeper hardpan layer, the claypan serves to hold water in the vernal pool.

Water in vernal pools is ultimately lost to slow infiltration and evaporation, so they usually dry up in late spring. But it's just enough time for fairy shrimp, spadefoot toads, and other wetland critters to complete one life cycle. The gradual evaporation of water over a period of weeks leads to spectacular concentric displays of wildflowers. As the pool dries, more wildflowers emerge closer to the center of the pool. The peak wildflower display at Mather is usually in late April.

Vernal pool at Mather Regional Park

29. LAKE TAHOE
History of a Basin

The Tahoe Basin is geologically young, having formed only a few million years ago. As the Sierra Nevada and Carson Range rose along vertical faults, the block of land between them dropped down, forming a valley. Later, eruptions from Mount Pluto, at the north end of Lake Tahoe, and other volcanoes dammed the northern outlet of the valley. With time, glaciers in the surrounding mountains formed and then melted, sending torrents of water into the basin. Today, sixty-three streams flow into the lake, but only one, the Truckee River, flows out, draining north into Pyramid Lake in Nevada.

The elevation of the surface of Lake Tahoe, currently more than 6,200 feet above sea level, is constantly changing due to fluctuations in rainfall, evaporation, runoff from surrounding mountains, and dam releases. With a maximum depth of 1,645 feet, Lake Tahoe is the second deepest lake in the United States (Oregon's Crater Lake is deeper), but both Crater Lake and Lake Tahoe pale in comparison to Siberia's Lake Baikal, which is more than 5,300 feet deep. Historically, Lake Tahoe's water level has been much higher than it is today. Ancient lake terraces indicate that it was about 800 feet higher a mere 10,000 years ago at the end of the last major glacial stage in this area.

Members of the Washoe Tribe lived sustainably at Lake Tahoe for centuries, but shortly after explorer John C. Frémont spied the lake in 1844, the secret was out. The Gold Rush, arrival of the trans-Sierra stagecoach in 1857, a Truckee railroad connection in 1900, and a land grab in the 1920s resulted in a population boom that stressed the lake's ecosystem. Throughout the 1950s and 1960s, construction of homes and communities filled in many of the lakeside wetlands that had functioned as natural filters for removing nitrogen, phosphorus, and iron from runoff before the water entered the

Emerald Bay in the southwestern part of Lake Tahoe

Underwater topography of Lake Tahoe. Color values range from red (shallow) to purple (deep). Emerald Bay is the small red ellipse near the southwest corner of the image. —Image courtesy of U.S. Geological Survey

lake. Without the buffering capacity of the wetlands, nutrient-rich runoff encouraged the growth of algae and other aquatic plants, diminishing the lake's legendary clarity.

One of the best places to learn about Lake Tahoe's geology and ecosystem is the U.S. Forest Service Taylor Creek Visitor Center in South Lake Tahoe. The Rainbow Trail, a half-mile loop, features a stream profile chamber that descends below the water level of Taylor Creek. Here, visitors can watch colorful rainbow trout swim past the viewing windows.

30. GROVER HOT SPRINGS STATE PARK
Sierra Volcanics

With fewer than 1,300 residents, Alpine is the least populated of California's fifty-eight counties. More than 90 percent of Alpine County is public land, including Grover Hot Springs State Park, which draws thousands of visitors each year to the park's hot pool and outdoor recreational opportunities. Located 4 miles west of Markleeville, the springs have been a popular tourist destination since the 1840s.

Grover Hot Springs is near one of the largest volcanic centers in the Sierra Nevada. This group of volcanic rocks, named the Markleeville Center, is 5 miles in diameter and consists of multiple intrusions of andesite and dacite that are about 6 million years old. This region is also crosscut by multiple faults, part of an active network of faults associated with ongoing uplift of the Sierra. The fault network opens pathways for hot groundwater, heated by residual heat from the ancient magma intrusions, to emerge at springs such as Grover Hot Springs.

The actual source pool at Grover Hot Springs is far too hot (148 degrees Fahrenheit) and too small to soak in, so the springwater is gravity-fed via a narrow wooden flume to a large concrete pool, where the temperature is maintained between 102 and 104 degrees Fahrenheit.

Algae-laden water from a hot spring flowing into a meadow at Grover Hot Springs State Park

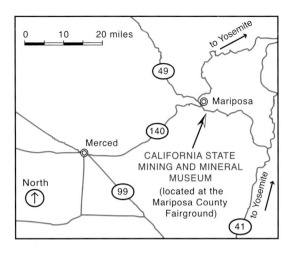

Samples of benitoite, the California state gemstone

Gold nuggets in a pan

31. CALIFORNIA STATE MINING AND MINERAL MUSEUM
Gemstones and Gold

Got gold? The California State Mining and Mineral Museum does. Located in Mariposa, the centerpiece of the museum's extensive collection of gems and minerals is the Fricot "Nugget," which amounts to almost 14 pounds of crystallized gold. This rare find looks like a small branching shrub, and we are lucky it wasn't melted down for the value of the gold.

The museum has a small-scale replica of an assay office, the place where the value of gold ore was determined. The rock samples were crushed to a fine powder, mixed to ensure uniformity, and then weighed. Powdered lead was added to the sample, which was then melted in the assayer's oven and poured into cone-shaped molds to cool. The melting lead collected all the valuable metals as it sank to the bottom of the cone. Once cool, the glassy "slag" was broken off and the mixture of gold and lead was further processed to pull out the lead. The remaining button of gold and silver was weighed, and then nitric acid was used to dissolve and wash away the silver, leaving only pure gold. The weight of the remaining gold, divided by the weight of the original rock sample, determined the gold content of the ore.

Included within the museum's twenty thousand mineral and rock specimens are several excellent examples of California's official state gemstone, benitoite, and economically significant minerals containing the elements copper, lead, zinc, silver, and platinum. There are also displays of meteorites and eerie-looking fluorescent minerals, which glow under ultraviolet light.

One of the highlights of a visit to the museum is walking through the 175-foot-long replica of a mine tunnel. It contains exhibits describing the mining process, including how explosives were used to blast away rock.

View of El Capitan (left), Half Dome (middle background), and Bridalveil Fall (right), in Yosemite National Park

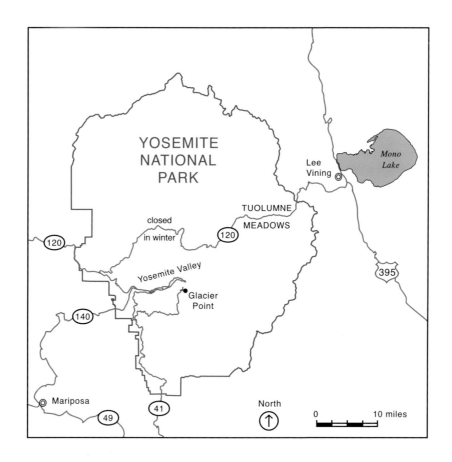

YOSEMITE
NATIONAL
PARK

Lee
Vining

*Mono
Lake*

TUOLUMNE

MEADOWS

closed
in winter

120

120

Yosemite Valley

395

Glacier
Point

140

Mariposa

North

0   10 miles

49

41

32. YOSEMITE NATIONAL PARK
Sculpting by Water and Ice

Erosion by water and ice over millions of years carved John Muir's "incomparable valley," the dramatic granitic landscape of Yosemite National Park. As the modern Sierra Nevada rose in the last 10 million years, it tilted up to the east. Rivers began to flow down the range's western slope, cutting valleys that were V-shaped in cross section, with slopes that were steep but not vertical. Yosemite Valley started to take shape as the ancestral Merced River cut downward. About 1 million years ago, during the Pleistocene Ice Ages, ice covered large portions of the Sierra Nevada and glaciers flowed westward down the valleys. As it flowed, the ice scraped off vast amounts of granite, slowly deepening and reshaping Yosemite Valley from a V-shaped river valley to a U-shaped glacial valley with nearly vertical walls.

At least two other glaciations have occurred in Yosemite during the past 200,000 years, but the 1-million-year-old Sherwin Glaciation was the most significant. After the glacier melted, smaller tributary rivers were left "hanging" above the deepened valley floor. Watercourses in those hanging valleys, such as Bridalveil and Yosemite Creeks, rush over the high walls of Yosemite Valley, forming spectacular waterfalls.

The huge glaciers that shaped Yosemite Valley are long gone, but rockfalls continue to modify the cliff faces today, leaving behind such distinctive features as the Three Brothers and the northwest face of Half Dome. One of the biggest Yosemite rockfalls in recent decades was in March 1987 on the slope below Three Brothers. Nearly 1.5 million tons of rock fell during this event, closing Northside Drive for months.

Rockfalls are the dramatic end result of weathering along surface fractures known as joints. These zones of weakness hasten erosion. There are several types of joints. A regional joint system is a set of parallel fractures formed by forces within Earth. Weathering along these joints dominates the formation of large-scale features. Exfoliation joints, also called "onion-skin weathering," are more localized. As erosion of overlying rock reduces pressure on deeply buried granite, it expands slightly and eventually breaks free, one layer at a time, giving the rock a layered appearance. Exfoliation weathering is responsible for the rounded shape of Yosemite's many domes,

including North Dome, Sentinel Dome, and the southeast side of Half Dome.

Tuolumne Meadows

The eastern entrance to Yosemite National Park is at 9,945-foot Tioga Pass, the highest road crossing of the Sierra Nevada. West of the pass, the road drops down to the 8,600-foot elevation of Tuolumne Meadows, where you can see glacially carved granite domes. Lembert Dome, the large whale-shaped rock that rises 800 feet over the east end of Tuolumne Meadows, is a type of glacial landform known as a roche moutonnée. This

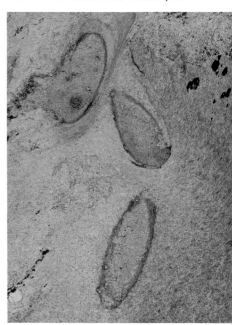

Oval potholes in Pothole Dome in Tuolumne Meadows

Large rectangular feldspar crystals in the Cathedral Peak Granodiorite of Pothole Dome

Exfoliation layers in granite in Yosemite

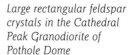

asymmetrical feature is smooth on one side and rough on the other because, as glacial ice moved from east to west over the rock, it flowed uphill, polishing and rounding a gentle slope, and then plucked loose rock from the steep downstream side. The smooth, shiny areas on Lembert Dome are glacial polish. As a glacier slides over granite, it smoothes the rock's surface with the help of sand embedded in the ice. Rocks embedded in the glacier carve grooves parallel to the direction of the glacier's flow.

Pothole Dome, the much smaller whale-shaped rock at the west end of Tuolumne Meadows, is also a polished roche moutonnée. Pothole Dome is named for potholes eroded by glacial meltwater flowing beneath the ice. Stones carried by a subglacial stream may be trapped and sloshed around in a rough area of the rock, eroding the surface, forming, and then polishing an ever-deepening pothole. Most of the potholes are located on the dome's steep southern face, just past the hairpin bend in the trail that winds around the west end of the meadow.

Lembert and Pothole Domes are composed of 86-million-year-old Cathedral Peak Granodiorite, one of hundreds of individual bodies of intrusive igneous rock in the Sierra Nevada. The granodiorite is notable for large, white, rectangular potassium feldspar crystals up to 3 inches long.

Lembert Dome in Tuolumne Meadows. The glacier moved from right to left, flowing up the gentle slope and plucking rocks from the steep slope.

A massive glacier flowing down the Kings River valley eroded the granitic rock of North Dome at Kings Canyon National Park.

light-colored minerals, potassium feldspar, plagioclase, and quartz. If the crystals are large enough, they can be identified in the field. Biotite, typically black or dark brown, breaks off in flat sheets because of its planar structure. Hornblende typically appears as black to dark green or brown crystals that may be rectangular or long and skinny. Potassium feldspar is typically opaque, has a white to pink color, and forms rectangular crystals. In granitic rocks rich in potassium feldspar, the crystals may be quite large, even several inches across. Plagioclase is typically translucent or opaque and white or gray and has rectangular crystals, and sometimes tiny, parallel lines. Quartz is typically translucent, gray, and shapeless. It is the last mineral to crystallize when a granitic mass is cooling, so it fills the space between all of the other crystals. Although granitic rocks can include other minerals, these five are the most common.

33. KINGS CANYON NATIONAL PARK
Mineralogy of Granite

Kings Canyon National Park lies surrounded by Sequoia National Park and the John Muir and Monarch Wilderness Areas, and, together, these federally protected lands hold one of the largest roadless areas in the continental United States. Kings Canyon is also a peak-bagger's paradise: thirty-one of the park's thirty-four major peaks exceed 11,000 feet elevation, and thirteen of those top out in the rarefied air above 13,000 feet.

Kings Canyon's high peaks are the targets of hundreds of lightning strikes during summer thunderstorms. This makes them good places to find fulgurites, rocks melted from the heat of lightning strikes, which can form small glassy, burnt, or scorched areas on otherwise normal-looking rocks. Sand fulgurites, hollow tubes of fused particles, may form when lightning strikes sand.

The granitic rocks in Kings Canyon National Park, like other granitic rocks throughout the Sierra, consist primarily of two dark-colored minerals, biotite and hornblende, and three

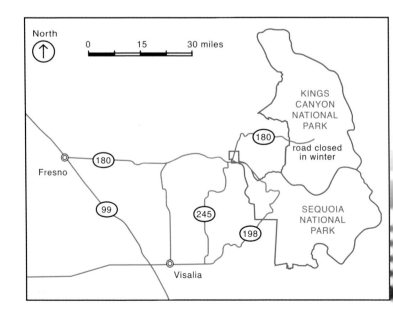

34. SEQUOIA NATIONAL PARK
Caves in Marble

Despite California's vast geologic diversity, it has relatively few limestone caverns, but in Kings Canyon and Sequoia National Parks, there are many caves formed in marble. The marble of Crystal Cave, in Sequoia National Park, originated as an ancient coral, part of a sequence of layers that included sand and mud. Through time, the coral, sand, and mud layers hardened, forming limestone, sandstone, and shale. When these rocks were deeply buried by further deposition, the heat and pressure turned the limestone, sandstone, and shale into the metamorphic rocks marble, quartzite, and schist, all evident today in the landscape near Crystal Cave.

Limestone and marble are made of calcium carbonate, which dissolves in naturally occurring carbonic acid, formed as snowmelt and rainwater absorb carbon dioxide from the atmosphere and soil. Over time, the acid dissolves the soluble rock along cracks, forming narrow channels, some of which become caves large enough for people to explore, including Crystal Cave, which is open to the public.

When carbonic acid dissolves calcium carbonate, it forms calcium bicarbonate in the water. On reaching an open cavern, the calcium bicarbonate solution releases its carbon dioxide, leaving behind calcium carbonate crystals in the form of stalactites, stalagmites, and other related cave features.

In time, the exceedingly slow deposition of calcium carbonate from the ceiling of a cavern will form a stalactite. In Crystal Cave, it's estimated that each inch of stalactite takes three hundred years to form. Stalagmites form when calcium bicarbonate solution from a stalactite drips onto the floor of a cavern. Stalagmites and stalactites may eventually merge, forming a column. An easy way to remember the difference between a stalactite and a stalagmite is that a stalactite holds "tight" to the ceiling.

Stalactites, stalagmites, and a column in Crystal Cave

Crystal Cave in marble

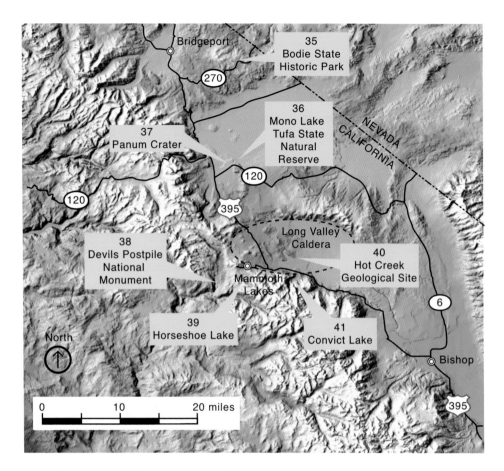

Bridgeport

270

37
Panum Crater

35
Bodie State
Historic Park

36
Mono Lake
Tufa State
Natural
Reserve

NEVADA
CALIFORNIA

120

120

395

Long Valley
Caldera

38
Devils Postpile
National
Monument

Mammoth
Lakes

40
Hot Creek
Geological Site

6

39
Horseshoe Lake

41
Convict Lake

Bishop

North

0   10   20 miles

395

EASTERN SIERRA

Vertical faulting along the eastern side of the Sierra has produced thousands of feet of uplift, creating one of the most distinctive escarpments in the United States. The steep topography is particularly prominent in the southern Sierra. From Lone Pine to the lofty summit of Mount Whitney, the highest mountain in the continental United States, the elevation increases nearly 10,600 feet in a horizontal distance of only 13 miles. The east side of the Sierra is also home to Long Valley Caldera, the remnants of a massive volcanic eruption that occurred some 760,000 years ago. The blast sent over 140 cubic miles of volcanic rock and ash aloft, and some of it eventually landed as far east as present-day Nebraska. The Long Valley eruption was nearly five hundred times larger than the 1980 eruption of Mount Saint Helens in Washington. The huge depression that remains, an oval-shaped area extending approximately 11 by 18 miles, is still geologically active today. Hot springs well up within the cold current of Hot Creek, carbon dioxide emissions kill trees on the slopes of Mammoth Mountain, and the resurgent dome within the caldera continues to expand, having risen more than 2 feet since 1980.

35. BODIE STATE HISTORIC PARK
Gold Mining Ghost Town

Bodie State Historic Park, featuring a gold- and silver-mining ghost town, is located southeast of Bridgeport. Although W. S. Bodey (one of several spellings) discovered gold here in 1859, it would be almost two decades before gold fever drew nearly ten thousand residents to this remote eastern Sierra outpost, situated at 8,300 feet. The town thrived from 1877 to 1882, and more than $30 million worth of gold in 1880 dollars was extracted from its network of mines. Although most Californians equate gold with the Mother Lode Country on the western slope of the Sierra, gold has been mined commercially in forty-seven of California's fifty-eight counties. Bodie was one of the most significant deposits mined during the late 1800s.

At least two major fires destroyed much of Bodie, but about two hundred structures remain. The town's population dwindled in the 1940s, finally being reduced to a lone caretaker until it became a state park in 1962. The park is maintained in a state of arrested decay, and several buildings are propped up with posts to keep them from falling over. Visitors are encouraged to wander freely through town, and park rangers conduct guided tours of the stamp mill, which houses huge machines used to pound ore into fine particles so that gold could be extracted.

The gold at Bodie is an epithermal deposit related to ancient volcanic activity in the region. Epithermal deposits form when mineral-rich water from deep underground rises along fractures in the rock and then cools, precipitating the minerals in veins near the surface. At Bodie, the principal ore-bearing quartz vein was approximately 1,000 feet wide and 1,000 feet deep.

Stamp mill at Bodie State Historic Park

Bodie, a ghost town

Light-colored Paoha Island (background) *and tufa limestone* (right foreground) *at Mono Lake*

36. MONO LAKE TUFA STATE NATURAL RESERVE
Pillars of Limestone

In 1941, the city of Los Angeles diverted water from four of the five freshwater creeks that feed Mono Lake for their urban water supply. By 1982, the lake had dropped 45 feet in elevation, losing half its volume and doubling in salinity. The lake was dying, but a grassroots effort fought to save it. At Mono Lake's South Tufa visitor site, the short paved trail from the parking lot ends at an elevation of 6,392 feet, the restoration level mandated by the Water Resources Control Board in 1994. Below that elevation, a plank boardwalk continues down to the edge of the lake. In 2009, the lake's elevation stood at 6,382 feet, still 10 vertical feet from the restoration level. As the lake level rises, park rangers will remove boards from the lake end of the boardwalk. When they remove the last nail from the last board in the South Tufa boardwalk, the restoration of Mono Lake will be a success. Although still 25 feet lower than the lake's level prior to diversion, 6,392

feet is an elevation that biologists believe will stabilize the ecosystem.

The most striking features of Mono Lake are the tufa towers, craggy limestone pillars best seen at South Tufa. The limestone in tufa is produced as freshwater springs bubble up from the lake bottom. The calcium-rich springwater interacts with the carbonate-rich lake water and forms hard calcium carbonate (limestone). Tufa towers are continuously forming within Mono Lake. The towers visible at South Tufa are indicative of the lake's former water level, since tufa only forms underwater. Research at similar lakes in Nevada suggests that tufa may have fast growth rates, exceeding 1 inch per year. While this may seem slow, it's quite fast compared to the growth of calcium carbonate cave features, which may take a century or more to grow 1 inch.

At nearby Navy Beach, delicate sand tufa formations line the shore. Sand tufa forms when calcium-rich springwater wells up through Mono Lake's sandy bottom, forming a weak calcium carbonate cement that holds the sand grains together.

37. PANUM CRATER
A Very Recent Eruption

Panum Crater is a brief side trip near Mono Lake's South Tufa site; look for a very small sign to Panum on California 120 approximately 2.9 miles east of the US 395 intersection. Located at the end of a short three-quarter-mile gravel road, Panum is the youngest of the Mono Crater chain of small rhyolite volcanoes, having erupted only 650 years ago. Rhyolite is an extrusive igneous rock with the same composition as granite, but because the magma reached the surface and solidified quickly into a volcanic rock, it is rhyolite. Because rhyolite lava has lots of silica, gas gets trapped in it, making rhyolite eruptions quite explosive.

Panum's central dome is surrounded by a ridge of tephra, volcanic ash and fragments deposited from the air. Much of the rock inside the crater consists of obsidian and pumice, which are both chemically similar to rhyolite but cool so quickly that crystals don't have a chance to develop. Pumice is a very gassy, frothy variation of rhyolite. Typically light gray in color, pumice contains so much entrapped air that it's less dense than water and therefore floats.

Obsidian is a glassy black or gray rock that has very sharp edges when broken. Native Americans made obsidian into tools and arrowheads. Shaping obsidian takes years of practice, as well as plenty of protective equipment because the obsidian shards are, literally, as sharp as broken glass.

Eastern Sierra (background), *a ridge of volcanic ash and fragments* (middle), *and obsidian* (foreground) *in the center of Panum Crater*

Close-up of obsidian

38. DEVILS POSTPILE NATIONAL MONUMENT
Columns in a Lava Flow

Devils Postpile formed approximately 100,000 years ago when a series of immense lava flows filled a narrow valley to a depth of 400 feet. Cracks in the cooling lava radiated out at nature's preferred angle of 120 degrees, meeting up with other fractures to form the hexagonal pillars known as columnar jointing. Although six-sided columns are the most common, the pillars at Devils Postpile range from three-sided to seven-sided. The natural space-saving angle of 120 degrees can also be found in the structure of a honeycomb, a tortoise's shell, and even corn on the cob.

Devils Postpile (closed in winter) has a mandatory shuttle bus system during the summer. After a harrowing ride down a steep one-lane road, the bus makes several stops on the narrow valley floor where Devils Postpile is located. The main Devils Postpile outcrop is less than a half-mile walk from a shuttle bus stop. From the base of the outcrop, another trail leads to the top, affording a cross-sectional view of the columnar jointing. At the top you can also see glacial striations, parallel gouges in the rock surface that formed when debris-encrusted ice slid over the surface. As impressive as Devils Postpile is, what visitors see is only a small fraction of the original 3-mile-long lava flow. Over the millennia since the flow cooled, erosion by glaciers and river has removed the rest of the columns.

The glacially polished top of the columns at Devils Postpile

Columns at Devils Postpile National Monument

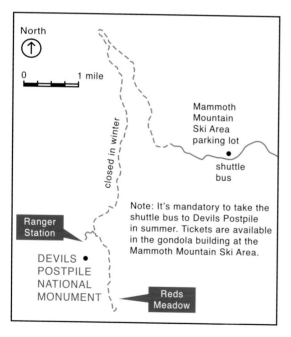

North ↑

0   1 mile

closed in winter

Mammoth Mountain Ski Area parking lot

● shuttle bus

Note: It's mandatory to take the shuttle bus to Devils Postpile in summer. Tickets are available in the gondola building at the Mammoth Mountain Ski Area.

Ranger Station

DEVILS ●
POSTPILE
NATIONAL
MONUMENT

Reds Meadow

39. HORSESHOE LAKE
Carbon Dioxide Tree Kill

In the early 1990s, Horseshoe Lake, southwest of the community of Mammoth Lakes, was the site of a scientific mystery. Researchers were stymied by the die-off of lodgepole pine after ruling out the usual suspects of insect infestation and drought. Additional investigations revealed the presence of very high concentrations of carbon dioxide in the soil at the site. The carbon dioxide damaged the fine structure of the tree roots, limiting their ability to take up water and nutrients, which led to the die-off.

The excessive carbon dioxide venting in the Horseshoe Lake area appears to be related to a 1989 swarm of earthquakes on the flanks of Mammoth Mountain, a silica-rich composite volcano formed by a series of eruptions between about 115,000 and 50,000 years ago. Magma rising from deep underground may have triggered the earthquakes. Possible sources of the carbon dioxide include off-gassing of the rising magma and gas release from heating of the limestone that lies below Mammoth Mountain. The U.S. Geological Survey continues to monitor seismic activity in the region and carbon dioxide emissions from Mammoth Mountain as part of the Long Valley Observatory program.

Trees killed by high concentrations of carbon dioxide in soil at Horseshoe Lake

40. HOT CREEK GEOLOGICAL SITE
Hot Geysers in a Cold Creek

Swimming in Hot Creek, an undeveloped hot springs, was once a de rigueur activity on any tour of Mono County. This activity was risky, however, because of sudden changes in water temperature and flow. Here, a series of hot springs bubble up from the streambed of a cold-water creek as it flows through the center of the Long Valley Caldera, the remnant of a massive volcanic eruption 760,000 years ago. However, the onset of dangerous geyser activity in 2006 forced a temporary closure of the creek to swimming or soaking because scalding water may erupt at any time. In geologic time, temporary is a very long time indeed, and Hot Creek is likely to remain closed indefinitely. When a geyser erupts, water in the seemingly placid creek can spurt up to 6 feet high, spewing scalding hot water on the unwary. U.S. Geological Survey researchers studying Long Valley Caldera haven't been able to tie the recent geyser activity to any specific geologic changes, but it may be related to long-term temperature increases in groundwater or possibly to a 1997 earthquake swarm that could have opened new pathways for geothermal water and steam.

Reflection of the sky on the white clay bottom of the Hot Creek pool causes the vivid blue color. Abundant nutrient support the algae growing in Hot Creek in lower foreground

Nearby, the California Department of Fish and Game's Hot Creek Fish Hatchery produces nearly 300,000 pounds of catchable fish and 14 million trout eggs annually. A small volume of thermal water (260 to 320 degrees Fahrenheit) and a larger volume of nonthermal water (50 degrees Fahrenheit) combine underground west of Hot Creek, resulting in water of a temperature and quality ideal for raising fish. This naturally mixed water is the source of the water in the springs (approximately 52 to 64 degrees Fahrenheit) that supply the hatchery.

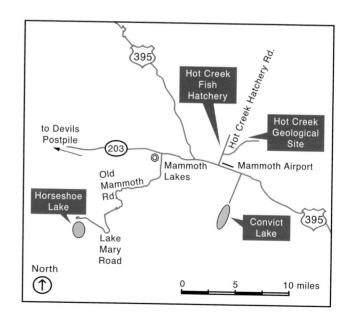

60

41. CONVICT LAKE
A Roof Pendant

Convict Lake, just a few miles south of the community of Mammoth Lakes, is one of the best locations to see California's older metamorphic rocks intruded by the granitic rock of the Sierra. Formed as continental rocks were melted by the heat produced by subduction of the Farallon Plate, the granite magma intruded into and engulfed the older metamorphic rocks. Later, uplift of the Sierra exposed both the metamorphic rock and the granite. The remnants of the older rocks are called roof pendants, named for the way they appear to hang down into the granitic body. Sevehah Cliff, at the southwest end of Convict Lake, is part of the Mount Morrison roof pendant, named for the high peak immediately south of Convict Lake. Strikingly beautiful in morning sunlight, Sevehah Cliff is a contorted riot of tan, gray, brown, orange, and white layers of tightly folded and faulted rocks.

The massive bulk of light gray rock in the central part of Sevehah Cliff is the Mount Morrison Sandstone. Although folded and faulted, the Mount Morrison Sandstone is more than 1,100 feet thick. The highly reflective bright white rock immediately below the gray rock is also Mount Morrison Sandstone. The white color is caused by alteration of the minerals calcite and quartz to wollastonite, a metamorphic mineral. The small orange outcropping immediately left of the wollastonite zone is the Aspen Meadow Formation, a silica-rich rock that weathers to orange. The distinctive chocolate brown layer immediately above the Mount Morrison Sandstone is chert and argillite, and part of the Squares Tunnel Formation. Argillite is a hard, fine-grained clay- and silica-rich rock. There are many other formations and faults present on the cliff, but they're difficult to discern from a distance.

The rocks forming Sevehah Cliff were marine sediments, probably deposited about 400 million years ago at the base of a continental slope in relatively deep water. Layers of sandstone were formed from sediments flowing down the continental slope into a submarine fan. The silica-rich rocks were deposited in deeper water, far from the continent, where the detritus of microscopic plankton built up layers of sediment over many millions of years.

Sevehah Cliff lit up by morning sun at the southwest end of Convict Lake

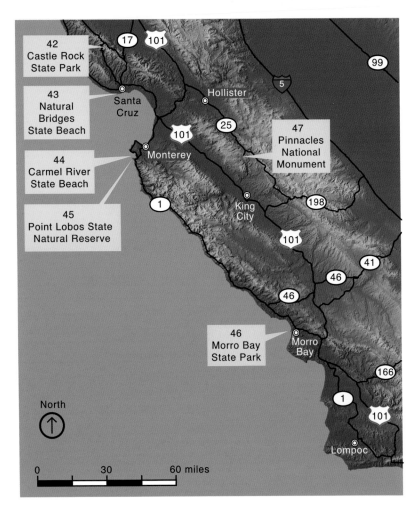

42
Castle Rock
State Park

43
Natural
Bridges
State Beach

44
Carmel River
State Beach

45
Point Lobos State
Natural Reserve

46
Morro Bay
State Park

47
Pinnacles
National
Monument

17 101

99

5

Hollister

Santa
Cruz

101

25

Monterey

1

King
City

198

101

41

46

46

Morro
Bay

166

1

101

Lompoc

North

0   30   60 miles

CENTRAL COAST

California's central coast, stretching from the Bay Area to
Santa Barbara, sports a dazzling array of geologic environments, from the steep edifice of Salinian Block granites in
the northern part of the Big Sur coastline to the more muted
contours of the Franciscan Complex in the south. Volcanic
rocks surface here and there, along with relatively young sedimentary rocks. And the pounding surf has shaped them all,
along with the largest coastal feature, the submarine Monterey
Canyon in Monterey Bay.

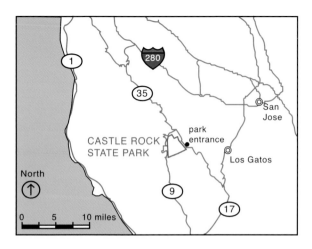

42. CASTLE ROCK STATE PARK
Tafoni Weathering of Sandstone

The Vaqueros Sandstone at Castle Rock State Park, located in the Santa Cruz Mountains, was deposited as sand some 30 to 20 million years ago in a shallow sea at the mouth of a river. Since then, tectonic movement along the San Andreas Fault system brought the Vaqueros Sandstone north to its current inland location. The pockmarks in the surface of the sandstone are a type of rock weathering called *tafoni* (singular: tafone). These pits and hollows in the rock surface may be caused by differential weathering and, possibly, differential cementation. Rain, which is naturally acidic, may dissolve the sandstone's calcium carbonate cement, the glue that holds individual sand grains together. The calcium carbonate migrates to the surface of the rock, forming a hard crust. The sandstone of the rock's interior is left relatively weak by the loss of calcium carbonate, creating pathways for erosion. When a small part of the cemented surface rock is weathered away, the interior weathers more quickly, forming holes.

Salt weathering may also be involved in the formation of tafoni, as they are frequently found in coastal areas and saline-rich desert environments. Salt may contribute to the weathering by chemical interactions with the rock matrix or

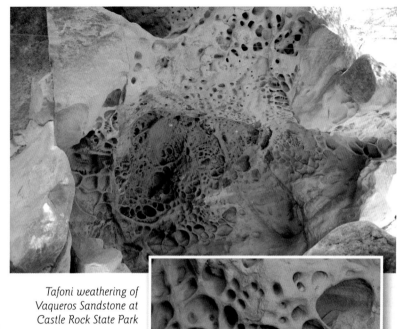

Tafoni weathering of Vaqueros Sandstone at Castle Rock State Park

by physical expansion of salt crystals during the crystallization process. Still another theory suggests that microclimates within each developing tafone are partly responsible. Air entering a shaded tafone condenses, allowing moisture to settle on the interior wall, which in turn advances the weathering. Several of the larger tafoni at Castle Rock State Park show a characteristic backward and upward weathering pattern, resulting in a miniature cavern that slopes upward as it retreats into the rock, supporting the microclimate theory.

43. NATURAL BRIDGES STATE BEACH
Coastal Erosion

Today, the name of this state beach should be Natural Bridge, not Natural Bridges. Once there were three, then there were two, and today only a single bridge remains. Natural bridges, or arches, are inherently unstable features; collapse is inevitable. A coastal natural bridge starts life as a promontory, a point of land that sticks out from the coast. Attacks are relentless. Waves pound against any small fracture or weak spot, and clams bore into the rock. Add in the erosive power of swirling sand carried in with each wave, and soon a small hollow spot forms, eventually becoming a sea cave. If the promontory is narrow enough, the sea cave may erode all the way through the rock, forming an arch.

Back around 1900, the three bridges at what was then Moore's Beach were still connected to the mainland. The outer bridge collapsed in the 1940s. In 1980, the connecting arch collapsed, leaving the remnant middle bridge seen today. Although most of the bridge consists of Miocene-age Santa Cruz Mudstone, the flat top of the bridge is a marine terrace that is approximately 105,000 years old.

Natural Bridges State Beach comes alive every fall with the onset of the monarch butterfly migration. Thousands of monarchs arrive in September and October to spend the winter in a small eucalyptus grove within the park. Although there are about one hundred wintering spots for monarchs in California, the Natural Bridges site is one of the largest.

Natural bridge at Natural Bridges State Beach

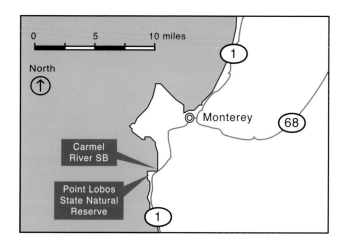

44. CARMEL RIVER STATE BEACH
Submarine Monterey Canyon

Monterey Canyon is comparable in size to the Grand Canyon but lies hidden underwater, on the seafloor. Carmel Canyon, one of the underwater tributaries feeding into the greater Monterey Canyon system, is a short swim out from Carmel River State Beach, and scuba divers have been exploring it for decades. Locally called Monastery Beach for the adjacent Carmelite Mission, Carmel River State Beach is one of the few places in California where experienced scuba divers can access very deep water from shore. However, the beach has a wickedly deceptive shore break that has proven fatal over the years.

Monterey Canyon, the biggest of several submarine canyons along the west coast of the United States, is a conduit for transporting sediment from the coast to the deep ocean. Sand from river outlets, beaches, and eroding cliffs migrates along the coast via longshore drift until it hits a sediment trap. When that trap is the head of a submarine canyon, the sand then flows down and out to the deep sea. The physics of longshore drift are simple. Incoming waves usually strike a beach at an angle. Sand entrained in the wave is forced up the beach at the same angle, but then gravity takes over and it flows back toward the ocean (in the wave's backwash) perpendicular to the shoreline. This constant out-and-back movement gradually sends sand along the shore.

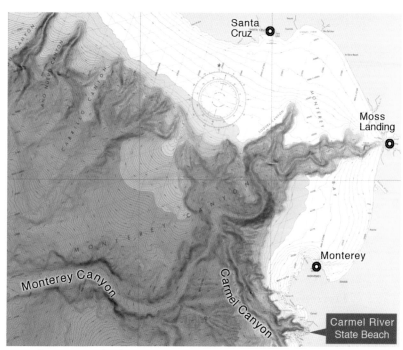

Seafloor topography showing Monterey Canyon and its tributary, Carmel Canyon —Image courtesy of the NOAA

Although the flow of sand into the head of the canyon is relatively continuous due to longshore drift, a vast volume of sediment can build up in the canyon's upper reaches until it either collapses under its own weight or is jarred loose by an earthquake. When that happens, there can be a massive underwater gravity flow, known as a turbidity current. As the loose sediments charge downslope, gravel and coarse sand move toward the base and the smallest particles (silts and clays) stay on top. The resulting sediment deposit, with coarse sediment at the bottom and fine grains on top, is called a turbidite. Since turbidity flows are relatively frequent events, turbidites usually contain a series of fining-up deposits, with each uppermost fine-grained layer overlain by the next coarse-grained layer that buried it. Franciscan Complex graywacke sandstone, which dominates California's North Coast, is an example of ancient turbidite deposits.

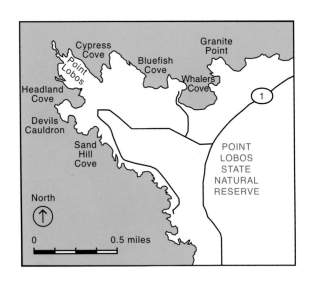

North

0   0.5 miles

45. POINT LOBOS STATE NATURAL RESERVE
The Salinian Block and the Carmelo Formation

Today's sea lions were called *lobos marinos*, or "sea wolves," by early Spanish settlers, giving rise to the name Punta de los Lobos Marinos for the rocky point south of Monterey. Erosion of two different rock types, the Santa Lucia Granodiorite, part of the larger 110- to 78-million-year-old Salinian Block, and the younger Carmelo Formation, a marine sedimentary rock, gives Point Lobos its craggy, rugged landscape. The Salinian Block, bracketed on the east by the San Andreas Fault and on the west by the Sur-Nacimiento Fault, dominates the

Santa Lucia Granodiorite at the tip of Point Lobos

northern part of the Big Sur coast and extends northward through Point Lobos State Natural Reserve and much of the Monterey Peninsula. The highly weathered granitic rocks of the Salinian Block frequently appear as crumbly outcrops with a salt-and-pepper texture. At Point Lobos, the Santa Lucia Granodiorite has particularly well-developed, white, rectangular crystals of potassium feldspar, generally 1 to 3 inches long. The granodiorite extends across the northern rocky cliffs of the reserve from Point Lobos to Granite Point and also outcrops at Bluefish Cove, Big Dome Cove, Cypress Cove, and Middle Cove. In the southern part of Point Lobos State Natural Reserve, the granodiorite crops out between Hidden and Gibson Beaches.

On the south side of Point Lobos State Natural Reserve, outcrops are mostly sedimentary rocks of the Carmelo Formation, a 1,000-foot-thick sequence of marine conglomerate, sandstone, and shale deposited on top of the older granodiorite. Conglomerate, a sedimentary rock containing rounded pebbles or cobbles, is deposited by fast-moving water. Trace fossils within the Carmelo Formation indicate these rocks were deposited some 60 to 50 million years ago approximately 600 to 1,500 feet below the water surface. This depth, along with the geometry of the deposit, indicates that the sediments were deposited by underwater landslides (turbidity currents) in a submarine canyon. In the intervening quiescent periods between slides, bottom-dwelling organisms burrowed into the sedimentary layers. Over time, the sediments solidified and were tectonically uplifted to their present-day elevation.

Within Point Lobos State Natural Reserve, rocks of the Carmelo Formation are most prominent at Sand Hill, Sea Lion, and Headland Coves, all on the south side of Point Lobos, and part of Whalers Cove, on the north side.

The Carmelo Formation closely resembles the Point Reyes Conglomerate. In fact, both may have been deposited in the same submarine canyon but were since separated by more than 100 miles due to offset along the San Gregorio and San Andreas Fault systems.

Carmelo Formation sedimentary rocks on the south side of Point Lobos State Natural Reserve. Waves have eroded the big trough in a weaker layer of the rock.

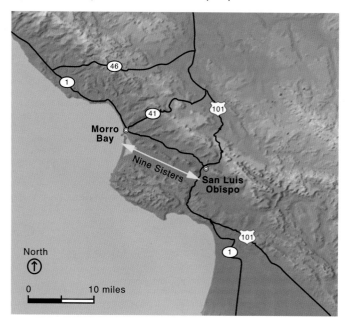

46. MORRO BAY STATE PARK
A Line of Volcanic Plugs

Morro Rock, a 576-foot-tall landmark that has guided mariners for centuries, is the best-known volcanic plug in a line of more than a dozen stretching from San Luis Obispo to Morro Bay. Nine of the most prominent peaks are known locally as the Nine Sisters. Strung out like a strand of pearls, these dacite volcanic plugs are the remnants of long-eroded volcanoes. A volcanic plug is a core of rock that solidifies from magma in the throat of a volcano when eruptions ceased. The Nine Sisters erupted from approximately 27 to 20 million years ago, probably along a fault.

To protect peregrine falcon habitat as well as other bird nesting sites and sensitive plant species, Morro Rock is off-limits to climbers, but visitors can walk around most of the base on a footpath. Of the other Sisters, several are privately owned and inaccessible, but Bishop Peak, Black Hill, Cerro Cabrillo, and Cerro San Luis Obispo all have hiking trails.

Morro Rock at Morro Bay State Park

Pinnacles of volcanic rock

*Bear Gulch Cave, talus cave
at Pinnacles National Monument*

47. PINNACLES NATIONAL MONUMENT
A Volcano Split by the San Andreas Fault

The rocks at Pinnacles National Monument, located about 80 miles south of San Jose, played a key role in our understanding of the San Andreas Fault. The eroded volcanic spires found at Pinnacles are the northern half of a larger volcanic complex that was split by the fault. The other half of the volcano, called Neenach, lies 195 miles southeast of Pinnacles, near the town of Lancaster in the Mojave Desert. The close geological match of the Pinnacles and Neenach volcanic rocks was used to confirm that both were part of the same eruptive event, which occurred approximately 23 million years ago. The current distance between them helped geologists determine how much movement has occurred along the San Andreas Fault.

The Pinnacles (and Neenach) rocks are a layered mix of high-silica volcanic material, including rhyolite, dacite, and andesite ash deposits. Deposits of tuff (sand-size volcanic fragments) and breccia (volcanic rocks embedded in tuff) are layered in with the ash. The high peaks are mainly made of breccia. Weathering and erosion of the weaker, less-resistant rocks and along fractures over the past 23 million years produced the sharp peaks and spires seen at Pinnacles National Monument today. Although it would be interesting to visit the Neenach outcrops, they are far less dramatic and are located on private land.

Pinnacles National Monument is home to a colony of Townsend's big-eared bats. They live in the park's talus caves, which are really just pockets and tunnels between large rocks that have collapsed together. Part of Bear Gulch Cave, the park's longest and most protected talus cave, is partially open most of the year, but the entire length of the half-mile-long cave is only open for a few weeks in fall when the Townsend's bat colony isn't in residence.

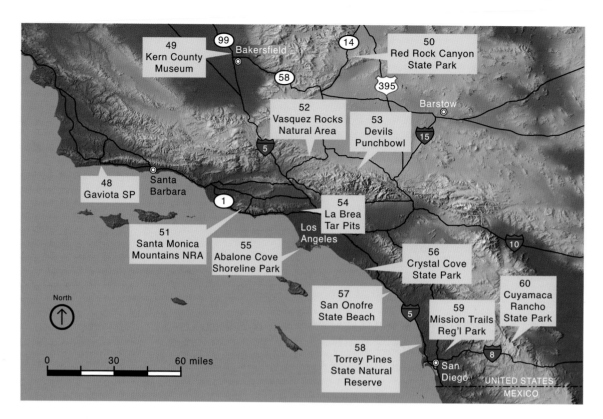

SOUTH COAST

The southern coastal region of California, which stretches from Santa Barbara to San Diego, includes some of the state's oddest mountains, the Transverse Ranges, which are nearly perpendicular to California's dominant northwest-southeast-trending mountains, such as the Sierra Nevada. The east-west trend is a product of the messy transition from a convergent plate boundary with a subduction zone to the current transform boundary, the San Andreas Fault.

Nearly 40 million years ago, California's western edge still butted up against the Farallon Plate, which was sliding very slowly beneath the less dense North American Plate in a process called subduction. About 30 million years ago, as the Farallon Plate was consumed, the Pacific Plate came into contact with the North American Plate, and the boundary between the plates changed from convergent, with subduction, to transform. The transition took millions of years and left several large blocks of Earth stuck between the plate margins. The Transverse Ranges were one such block. Originating near present-day San Diego, the entire block migrated northwest and rotated slowly clockwise to arrive in its current position.

Continental stretching associated with plate movement opened channels to magma deep within the Earth, resulting in volcanic eruptions within the Transverse Ranges. Later in their tectonic evolution, the Transverse Ranges were squeezed and uplifted by movement between the North American and Pacific Plates, particularly along a 50-mile stretch of the San Andreas Fault known as the Big Bend, in the Tehachapi Mountains. Here, the fault is oriented primarily west-east rather than northwest-southeast.

48. GAVIOTA STATE PARK
The Monterey Formation

Gaviota State Park, in Santa Barbara County, is a great place to explore the steeply dipping sedimentary rocks of the Santa Ynez Mountains. The youngest rocks in the park, at the coastline, are shale layers of the Monterey Formation, which is widespread across much of southern California. This economically important, oil-bearing unit formed between about 19 and 5 million years ago. This very fine-grained sedimentary rock varies in resistance across California, but in Gaviota State Park, especially near the pier, it is hard, brittle, and rich in silica. The constant rain of diatoms, single-celled phytoplankton with silica cell walls, built up over millions of years on the seafloor, producing the brittle, silica-rich portions of the Monterey Formation. Weathering along bedding layers and fractures in this rock produces distinctive rectangular or trapezoid-shaped blocks of hard shale.

The bedding of the Monterey Formation is parallel to the coast, so if you walk inland away from the beach, you'll pass through older bands of sedimentary rock extending east-west through the northern reaches of Gaviota State Park. Nearly all of the rocks tilt toward the south at moderate to steep angles, ranging from 30 to more than 80 degrees. The sedimentary units include marine shale of the Rincon Formation and shallow marine sandstone of the Vaqueros Formation. The Rincon Formation weathers to form low, rounded hillsides, while the more resistant Vaqueros Formation forms hard gray outcrops. Farther north are the older, nonmarine layers of the Sespe Formation: sandstone, siltstone, and claystone, including red beds created by oxidation of iron-bearing minerals within the sediment. Uphill from the Sespe Formation are the still older Alegria and Gaviota Formations, shallow marine sandstone, siltstone, and claystone deposited during a period of falling sea level. North of the Alegria-Gaviota sequence is the Sacate Formation, marine shale layers that are the oldest rocks in the park, ranging from approximately 37 to 34 million years old.

Silica-rich portions of the Monterey Formation weather to blocks.

Steeply dipping beds of the Monterey Formation parallel the coast at Gaviota State Park.

71

49. KERN COUNTY MUSEUM
Black Gold

A major exhibit at the Kern County Museum tells the story of oil in California. In Kern County, most of the oil formed from the organic matter in phytoplankton and zooplankton, minute marine plants and animals that lived millions of years ago, when a vast sea filled what is now the San Joaquin Valley. As the plankton died, they collected on the seafloor and were buried under thousands of feet of sediment. As these deposits were lightly heated deep underground, the hydrocarbon-containing organic compounds eventually separated out to form oil. The oil-rich Monterey Formation is the source rock of much of Kern County's oil.

Since oil is less dense than the rock that surrounds it, it tends to migrate upward. Where it reaches the surface, it bubbles out of the ground from what are known as *oil seeps*, which are found in many parts of California, including McKittrick in Kern County, Santa Paula in Ventura County, and La Brea Tar Pits in Los Angeles. The only way oil remains belowground is if it is trapped beneath rock or sediments of low permeability, such as clay. The rock the oil is trapped *within*, called the reservoir, is typically sandstone or limestone, which are very permeable.

One type of common geologic oil trap in California is an anticline, which is an A-shaped fold in the rock. Oil tends to migrate to the top of an anticline (the peak of the A), where it's trapped if the layer above the reservoir rock is sufficiently impermeable to contain the oil. Another common type of oil trap in California is a stratigraphic trap, where the reservoir rock lies between layers of less permeable rocks. Faults can also trap oil. If movement on the fault forces a less permeable rock over the reservoir rock, upward movement of oil is impeded. Fault gouge, clay formed in a fault zone by rocks grinding past each other, can also act as a trap.

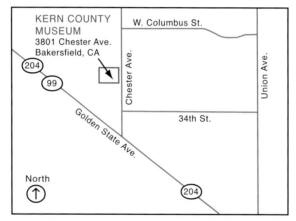

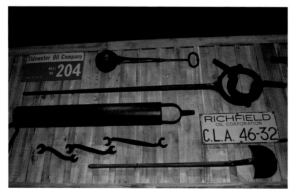

Early oil industry tools on display at the Kern County Museum   *Oil derrick at the Kern County Museum*

50. RED ROCK CANYON STATE PARK
Miocene Fossils

Travelers driving north on California 14 from the town of Mojave are treated to a stunning view of the colorful cliffs of Red Rock Canyon State Park. The red, pink, gray, and tan layers, part of the Dove Spring Formation in the Ricardo Group, were deposited 12 to 7 million years ago in a mountain basin near an active volcano. Layers of sedimentary rocks deposited in streams, floodplains, and lakes are interspersed with lava flows and other volcanic deposits. A vast array of mammal fossils, ranging from horse and camel to rhinoceros, beaver, skunk, hedgehog, shrew,

Dove Spring Formation of the Ricardo Group at Red Rock Canyon State Park, with a large fallen block in the foreground and basalt on the ridgetop (upper left corner)

squirrel, kangaroo rat, gopher, and fox, have been preserved in these rocks. Plant fossils, as well as fish and reptile fossils, also occur. The horses and camels were the most abundant large mammals, prey for the saber-toothed cats and bone-crushing dogs whose fossils have also been identified at Red Rock Canyon. Fossils discovered here are on display at the Los Angeles County Natural History Museum.

In the cliffs, fluted gray to tan columns appear to prop up higher layers of hard rock. The columns are carved in floodplain deposits, which are softer than overlying layers and thus more susceptible to erosion. The hard red rock, a conglomerate, consists of gravel and cobble stream channel deposits that contain iron-rich minerals. When exposed to air, iron

is oxidized to iron oxide, or rust. Other noteworthy layers include the black basalt flows, which are most prominent as the top layer on the west side of California 14 and along the entrance road to the park (Abbott Drive). The basalt, which erupted from a volcano about 10 million years ago, contains vesicles, holes left by gas bubbles trapped in the lava as it cooled and hardened. The pink layer of hard rock most visible along the east side of California 14 is tuff breccia, a mixture of tiny fragments of volcanic ash and larger pieces of rock ejected from the erupting volcano. As tuff settles out of the sky, the hot fragments of volcanic ash and rock are welded together, forming a relatively erosion-resistant rock.

51. SANTA MONICA MOUNTAINS NATIONAL RECREATION AREA
Transverse Ranges

At more than 150,000 acres, Santa Monica Mountains National Recreation Area is one of the largest urban parks in the world. Part of the Transverse Ranges, the Santa Monica Mountains extend west out to sea, forming the four northern Channel Islands. One of the most widespread rock units in the recreation area is the Conejo Volcanics, erupted from a chain of volcanoes about 16 to 13 million years ago. The park's highest point, in the center of the volcanics, is Sandstone Peak, a misnomer, as it's made primarily of andesite. Volcanic rocks solidify as soon as they erupt, which allows little time for crystals to form. The tiny crystals that do form as the rock is cooling may resemble grains of sand, so it can be difficult to distinguish between a fine-grained volcanic rock and sandstone. Viewing a thin slice of rock (called a thin section) under a microscope allows geologists to differentiate between sandstone and volcanic rock. Under the microscope, sand grains in sandstone may range from angular to well-rounded, but they do appear as sand grains rather than well-formed crystals.

The Conejo Volcanics, which also include dacite and basalt lava flows, tuff, and volcanic breccia, extend across the inland part of Point Mugu State Park, Circle X Ranch, and the western part of Paramount Ranch. Many of the older volcanic rocks are pillow basalts, indicating that they erupted underwater. The younger volcanics here include airborne debris deposited on land.

Malibu Creek State Park, view looking west. Conejo Volcanics are on the left (south) side of the stream and Calabasas Formation sedimentary rocks are on the right (north).

The entire area was tilted up to the northeast, so the insides of the volcanoes are exposed near the coast. The magma intruded through the Topanga Formation, as evidenced by dikes. The Topanga Formation is exposed in several of the park units close to the coast, including the southern part of Point Mugu State Park, Charmlee Wilderness Park, and Solstice Canyon. Distinctive sedimentary rock units within Point Mugu State Park include thick-bedded marine sandstones likely deposited close to shore.

Sandstone and shale of the Calabasas Formation overlie the volcanics. You can see them at Malibu Creek State Park on the north side of the creek between the main parking lot and Century Lake. Rocks on the south side of Malibu Creek, including the dramatic Goat Buttes, are primarily basalt, andesite, and volcanic breccia of the Conejo Volcanics. Differential erosion at Malibu Creek State Park makes some layers stand out more than others, creating a dramatic landscape that has been popular with Hollywood producers.

The oldest rocks in Santa Monica Mountains National Recreation Area, located on the eastern edge of Topanga State Park, consist primarily of Santa Monica Slate. These rocks date to late Jurassic time, some 160 to 145 million years ago. Slate is a metamorphic rock formed when sedimentary rock (typically shale) was altered by increased temperature and pressure. As the original rocks were metamorphosed, the minerals within the rock grew parallel to each other, giving the rock a flat, laminated appearance, termed foliation. Santa Monica Slate is typically black to bluish gray, but frequently weathers to brownish gray in outcrops.

Point Mugu in Santa Monica Mountains National Recreation Area

52. VASQUEZ ROCKS NATURAL AREA
Red Conglomerates and Fanglomerates

The dramatic tilted sedimentary layers at Vasquez Rocks Natural Area have served as a backdrop to many TV westerns, such as *Bonanza* and *Gunsmoke*, and movies, such as *Star Trek*, *Blazing Saddles*, and *Planet of the Apes*. The rocks exposed here are part of the Vasquez Formation, deposited about 30 million years ago on the slopes of mountains that have long since eroded away. The sedimentary layers include claystone, siltstone, sandstone, conglomerate, and fanglomerate. The conglomerates were former stream channel deposits. As rocks tumble downstream, their sharp edges are worn off, resulting in cobbles that are quite rounded. Fanglomerates, by contrast, are deposited in alluvial fans, which form in desert environments when seasonal flash flooding sends massive amounts of rubble downstream from steep mountain ranges. Rocks in fanglomerates are usually angular to subrounded because they haven't been subject to years of rolling around in a streambed.

The rocks here were uplifted and tilted because of movement along the San Andreas Fault, which lies just 8 miles northeast of Vasquez Rocks. Now exposed to erosion, the more resistant sandstones, conglomerates, and fanglomerates jet out of the land surface, some extending up to 150 feet high.

The rocks at Vasquez are red because they contain iron oxide. Although rocks may be red for a variety of reasons, the color often indicates that the rock was formed from sediments deposited on land in an environment with plenty of oxygen, rather than underwater.

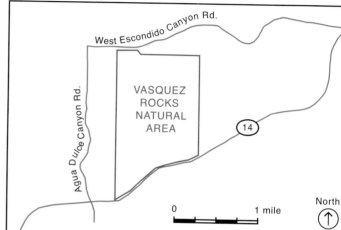

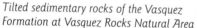
Tilted sedimentary rocks of the Vasquez Formation at Vasquez Rocks Natural Area

53. DEVILS PUNCHBOWL COUNTY PARK
Folded and Faulted Rocks

Devils Punchbowl County Park, on the north side of the San Gabriel Mountains, includes wonderful outcrops of folded and faulted sedimentary rock in its 1,300 acres. About 60 million years ago, sand, silt, and clay washed into a shallow sea here, building up layers that eventually hardened to form sandstone and shale of the San Francisquito Formation. Later, between about 60 and 40 million years ago, these rocks were folded and faulted by movement along the now-inactive Piñon Fault and several other related faults.

About 13 million years ago, streams flowing in from the north and west washed huge volumes of the eroded San Francisquito Formation downslope, where they settled in layers on top of other eroded San Francisquito rocks. These young sediments are the Punchbowl Formation, composed of rounded cobbles and angular fragments of rock in a sandy matrix. Later, movement along the San Andreas Fault, located just 3 miles to the north, and the Punchbowl Fault, which runs through the park along the north side of the San Gabriel Mountains, folded and faulted both the Punchbowl Formation and the older San Francisquito Formation. The older granitic rocks and metamorphic rocks of the San Gabriel Mountains rose up along the Punchbowl Fault, so the younger Punchbowl Formation is now in fault contact with these older rocks in the southern part of the park.

One of the most dramatic folds, a syncline with steeply tilted limbs, wraps around the Loop Trail. A syncline is a trough-shaped fold in which rock layers dip inward toward the center of the fold. Rocks on the north limb of the fold dip at angles of 30 to 50 degrees toward the southwest, while the rocks on the south side are much steeper, dipping 60 to 80 degrees to the northwest. The San Gabriel Mountains block much of the urban night light of Los Angeles, so the park is a good place to observe stars and meteor showers.

The steeply dipping Devils Punchbowl Formation at Devils Punchbowl County Park

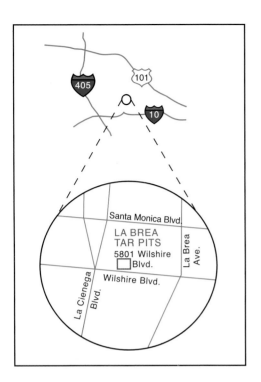

Today, the La Brea Tar Pits have far more value as a fossil repository, having yielded over one million bones representing more than two hundred different species, including mammoths, ground sloths, and California's state fossil, the saber-toothed cat, with its 7-inch fangs and powerful limbs. Most of the fossils date to the last Ice Age, about 40,000 to 10,000 years ago. One unique feature of La Brea is the high ratio of predator to prey animals found there. It's thought that a single entrapped prey animal, such as a mammoth, could have attracted a dozen or more predators, such as wolves, which then also became stuck in the muck. Because the tar pits were trapping animals over a 30,000-year time frame, it's estimated that the entrapment of only ten or so animals each decade could have produced the volume and density of fossils found in the tar pits.

54. LA BREA TAR PITS
Ice Age Fossils

Long before the La Brea Tar Pits were recognized for the wealth of fossils entombed in them, they were the dominant source of roofing tar for the rapidly growing city of Los Angeles. In the 1865 publication *Geology, Volume 1: Report of the Progress and Synopsis of the Field-Work from 1860 to 1864*, Josiah Whitney described it thus: "Over a space of fifteen or twenty acres, the bituminous material . . . was oozing out of the ground at numerous points. It hardens on exposure to the air, and becomes mixed with sand and dust blown into it, and is then known as 'brea.' . . . The brea is used almost exclusively for covering roofs at Los Angeles, selling (in 1861) at the springs for $1 per barrel, the purchaser collecting it himself, which is done by digging a pit two or three feet deep by the side of one of the holes from which the tar is issuing, and letting it fill up."

Saber-toothed cat skeleton at La Brea Tar Pits

Gas bubbles and oil sheen at La Brea Tar Pits

Sedimentary layers dipping toward the ocean at Abalone Cove Shoreline Park

55. ABALONE COVE SHORELINE PARK
Landslides

Abalone Cove Shoreline Park, located within the city of Rancho Palos Verdes, is an 80-acre package of tide pools, high cliffs, endangered plants, and a landslide. The Abalone Cove landslide is one of three related slides in the area, the largest of which is the infamous Portuguese Bend, just southeast of Abalone Cove. The Portuguese Bend landslide, which dates back at least 37,000 years, was reinvigorated in the mid-1950s and wrecked nearly one hundred homes in 1956 over the course of the year. The landslide has slowed considerably since then, from 1 to 5 inches of sliding per day to less than 1 inch per day, but it still wreaks havoc on local infrastructure, necessitating aboveground routing of utilities and near-constant road maintenance.

The landslide-prone geology of Abalone Cove and Portuguese Bend has its roots in the type and orientation of the sedimentary rocks in the area. Sedimentary layers deposited over millions of years were uplifted and tilted by tectonic activity and now dip south toward the shoreline, which runs east-west here. One of the sedimentary layers is a 40- to 70-foot-thick layer of volcanic ash known as the Portuguese Tuff. The ash has weathered to form a type of clay that gets very slippery when wet. Under the force of gravity, the tilted rocks slide toward the ocean along this plane of weakness.

In many landslides, the catalyst for ground movement is excessive subsurface water. Mitigation efforts typically include drilling wells to remove the water. This has been largely successful in stabilizing the Abalone Cove slide but less so at Portuguese Bend.

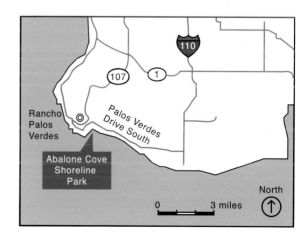

56. CRYSTAL COVE STATE PARK
Marine Terraces

Crystal Cove State Park and the adjacent Laguna Coast Wilderness Park encompass more than 9,000 acres of open space in Orange County, stretching from offshore to the top of the San Joaquin Hills, nearly 1,200 feet above sea level. In the intertidal zone, the Monterey Formation creates a rugged reef that provides numerous tide pools for anemones, sea stars, and hermit crabs. Scuba divers exploring the reef farther offshore may see halibut, garibaldi, sea bass, and bat rays in the kelp forest.

The coastal section of Crystal Cove State Park is a classic marine terrace, a relatively flat coastal plain left high and dry due to several different influences. The marine terraces in the coastal region from Newport Beach to Laguna Beach, which bracket Crystal Cove to the north and south, are likely the result of tectonic uplift of coastal southern California from about 413,000 to 120,000 years ago. Climate also played a role in stranding these terraces above the ocean's surface. Sea level has been both higher and lower than it is today, in part due to climate changes during globally cool periods (ice ages) and warmer periods (interglacial periods).

Inland of Crystal Cove, the San Joaquin Hills rise steeply in a series of marine and nonmarine folded and faulted sedimentary units, primarily medium- to coarse-grained sandstone. The ubiquitous Miocene-age Monterey Formation, widespread in southern California, cuts across the coastal hills in many places, with typically white to pale brown thinly layered siltstone and sandstone.

Monterey Formation sedimentary rock dipping toward the ocean at Crystal Cove State Park

A marine terrace in the distance sloping toward the sea

57. SAN ONOFRE STATE BEACH
Cristianitos Fault

The Cristianitos Fault cuts the beachside cliff at San Onofre State Beach just a short distance south of the San Onofre Nuclear Generating Station. The facility's designers investigated the fault prior to construction and determined that it's no longer active.

At San Onofre State Beach, the light-colored marine sandstone of the San Mateo Formation lies north of the fault and a tilted, interbedded claystone and siltstone sequence of the Monterey Formation lies south of it. The fault cuts through the cliff at the very north end of a landslide but is not well exposed. The San Mateo Formation is approximately 5 million years old, while the Monterey Formation dates to about 19 to 5 million years ago. Vertical movement along the Cristianitos Fault brought the older Monterey Formation upward, into contact with the younger San Mateo Formation.

A thick sequence of marine boulders and reddish brown terrestrial alluvium, which overlies both the San Mateo and Monterey rocks, is not cut by the Cristianitos Fault, indicating that movement along the fault ceased before the boulders and alluvium were deposited. Age dating of the boulder and alluvium indicates that this deposit is at least 125,000 years old, so the Cristianitos Fault has been inactive for at least that long.

View to the north of alluvium and San Mateo Formation sandstone (left background), *a landslide deposit* (middle), *and Monterey Formation shale* (right foreground)

...ddish brown alluvium and a thin boulder ...er overlying the San Mateo Formation ...ndstone at San Onofre State Beach

58. TORREY PINES STATE NATURAL RESERVE
Sedimentary Features along the Beach Trail

The Beach Trail in Torrey Pines State Natural Reserve cuts through 48 million years of coastal sediments. From the trailhead at the top of the bluff, the path begins in the youngest rocks, red sandstone of the Linda Vista Formation, winds through the buff-colored Torrey Sandstone, and crosses into the oldest rocks, grayish green siltstone of the Delmar Formation.

The Linda Vista Formation, a hard red sandstone widespread in coastal San Diego County, forms a distinctive platform near the top of the Beach Trail. Red Butte is an excellent example of the Linda Vista Formation, which was deposited in Pleistocene time. The abundance of iron oxide in the formation accounts for its characteristic red color. The Linda Vista is more resistant to erosion than the older Torrey Sandstone

beneath it, so it forms a caprock at Red Butte and throughout much of the Kearny Mesa, Mira Mesa, and Clairemont Mesa neighborhoods of San Diego.

Descending below the cobble base of the Linda Vista Formation, hikers enter the Torrey Sandstone, which extends almost down to the beach. The boundary between the Linda Vista and the Torrey Sandstone is an unconformity, a break in the rock record, in this case reflecting a 40-million-year gap in the geologic record. The Torrey Sandstone was eroded prior to deposition of the Linda Vista Formation.

The Torrey Sandstone is buff-colored, fine- to medium-grained sandstone with few fossils but many crossbeds—thin sandstone layers that cross the main bedding direction. Crossbeds are indicative of sand movement via air, as with sand

Red Butte of the Linda Vista Formation along the Beach Trail at Torrey Pines State Natural Reserve

dunes, or by water, as with waves. In the case of sand dunes, individual sand grains are swept up the windward face of a dune and then tumble down the leeward face. The same principle occurs in water deposition, but the crossbeds are usually much smaller. Most crossbeds in the Torrey Sandstone are quite small, typically only a few inches thick, which suggests water deposition, probably on a nearshore sandbar or barrier beach. Look for the crossbeds toward the lower end of the Beach Trail.

The Beach Trail ends at Flat Rock, a small wave-cut platform of the Delmar Formation that's about 5 feet high. The Delmar Formation, a grayish green, thinly bedded siltstone, is the most fossiliferous of the formations visible on the Beach Trail. Flat Rock contains numerous fossil clams and other shells typical of a lagoon or estuary environment, similar to the environment in the modern Penasquitos Lagoon, which is located immediately north of Torrey Pines State Natural Reserve.

Greenish gray Delmar Formation in Flat Rock (left foreground) *and buff-colored Torrey Sandstone* (right background) *at the end of the Beach Trail*

Crossbeds in the Torrey Sandstone along the Beach Trail

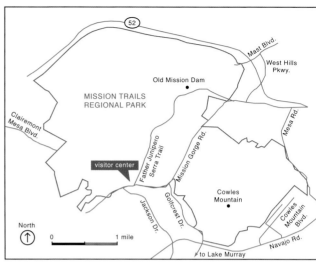

A mountain of granite at Mission Trails Regional Park.
—Photo by Susan Davis

59. MISSION TRAILS REGIONAL PARK
Mountain of Granite

Cowles Mountain, a granitic island in the sea of sedimentary rock that defines coastal San Diego County, dominates Mission Trails Regional Park. The 1.5-mile trail to the top of Cowles Mountain rewards hikers with a stunning 360-degree panoramic view of San Diego. The granitic rocks are a spur of the Peninsular Ranges, a chain of mountains extending from Los Angeles into Mexico. Like the granitic rock of the Sierra Nevada, the granitic rocks of the Peninsular Ranges solidified from magma produced by the heat generated by subduction of the Farallon Plate. Cowles Mountain is composed of granodiorite and tonalite, intrusive igneous rocks similar to granite but containing more plagioclase feldspar and less potassium feldspar than granite.

Lake Murray, also within Mission Trails Regional Park, is surrounded by a variety of interesting rocks, including an extensive outcrop of bouldery conglomerate, called the Stadium Conglomerate, on the north side of the lake. The Stadium Conglomerate was first named in Mission Valley near San Diego Stadium. The cobbles within the conglomerate are primarily the volcanic rocks dacite and rhyolite, washed downstream from an ancient volcano far to the east. Additional layers of conglomerate are embedded in the Mission Valley Formation, which hugs the southeast edge of Lake Murray. The Mission Valley Formation is predominantly a light grayish olive, fine- to medium-grained sandstone. The southwest edge of the lake, by contrast, abuts metamorphosed sedimentary and volcanic rocks.

60. CUYAMACA RANCHO STATE PARK
Rocks of the Peninsular Ranges

Cuyamaca Rancho State Park, located in the Cuyamaca Mountains (pronounced *kwee-ah-mah-ka*) east of San Diego, provides a great opportunity to examine the igneous and metamorphic rocks of the Peninsular Ranges. With elevations ranging up to 6,500 feet, this mountainous region provides a welcome respite from summer heat. The park's Stonewall Peak is part of the 113-million-year-old pluton called the Chiquito Peak Monzogranite. The pluton, a mass of igneous rock that cooled deep underground, is composed of granitic rocks containing five main minerals: potassium feldspar, plagioclase, quartz, biotite, and hornblende.

Distinctive light-colored dikes crisscross the granitic rock at the Green Valley Campground area. The dikes, which are several inches thick, formed when late-stage magma intruded cracks in the cooling igneous mass. Some of the dikes have large crystals, which typically increase in size toward the interior of the dike.

Cuyamaca Peak and Middle Peak are composed of early Cretaceous Cuyamaca Gabbro, an intrusive igneous rock that's the chemical equivalent of the volcanic rock basalt. Slow cooling of the Cuyamaca Peak Gabbro deep underground allowed the formation of large crystals of black hornblende, white plagioclase, and green olivine. Weathering of the iron-rich gabbro produces deep red soil.

Before it was a state park, the Cuyamaca area was one of the largest gold mining districts in San Diego County. Stonewall Mine, near the southwest corner of Lake Cuyamaca, was active in the late 1800s and produced approximately $2 million worth of gold during more than two decades of operation. The richest ore was located within a gold-bearing quartz zone inside the Triassic- to Jurassic-age Julian Schist, a metamorphic rock with a platy texture. Julian Schist also forms the upper part of Airplane Ridge, the erosion-resistant promontory that extends northwest from above Green Valley Campground.

View from Stonewall Peak, looking north toward Lake Cuyamaca and North Peak. —Photo by Kevin Key

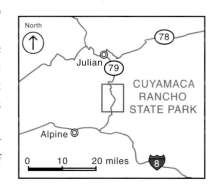

85

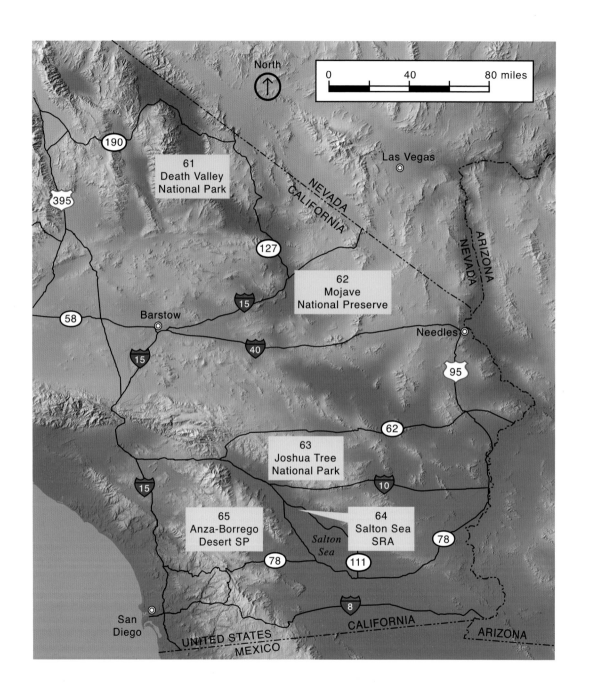

DESERTS

California's deserts are natural windows to the region's geologic features. Because of the lack of vegetation and soil cover, the rocks and landforms are easy to see. Young fault scarps cross alluvial fans, flash floods erode gullies, and wind blasts stones. Most of California's desert areas lie within the Basin and Range Province, a region that includes nearly all of Nevada and parts of California, Oregon, Idaho, Utah, Arizona, and New Mexico. This vast area, covering 200,000 square miles, is characterized by a succession of more than four hundred mountain ranges interspersed with basins, or valleys. The tectonic forces that created the Basin and Range date to about 20 million years ago, when stretching of the North American Plate caused the Earth's crust to thin and eventually fragment into hundreds of separate blocks, some of which dropped down while others rose up along faults. The Panamint and Amargosa Ranges, which bound Death Valley, are just two of the many uplifted, tilted blocks that define the Basin and Range Province. Between the mountains, the valleys are constantly being filled with sediments.

An alluvial fan in Death Valley

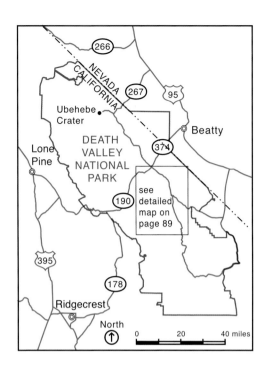

Salt spring at Devils Golf Course

61. DEATH VALLEY NATIONAL PARK
Salt Flats in a Closed Basin

The rugged landscape of Death Valley challenged early Gold Rush miners on their trek to California. Although the circuitous southern route to the Sierra goldfields was longer than the more direct route over the Sierra Nevada, it was a necessity for travelers who started too late in the season to avoid Sierra snows. The party that bestowed the grim name upon this valley lost only a single miner to the desert heat, but the name Death Valley remained. Like most basins of the Basin and Range Province, Death Valley is a closed basin, meaning it is completely enclosed by higher mountains and has no outlet to the sea. Water or snowmelt draining off the ranges flows toward low points in the valleys, where it infiltrates into the ground or forms shallow lakes. When the standing water evaporates, playas, or dry lakebeds, form and salts build up. Dozens of these lakebeds are scattered throughout southeastern California, including Searles, Cadiz, Panamint Flat, Lavic, Bristol, Danby, and Rogers Lakes.

Badwater, the lowest point in Death Valley at 282 feet below sea level, is also the lowest point in the United States. The salt flats at Badwater flood occasionally during times of high rainfall, but the water quickly evaporates. During periods of wetter climate in the past, particularly during the Pleistocene Ice Ages, Death Valley held a lake. As the climate warmed, the water evaporated, leaving behind Devils Golf Course, the rugged salt-encrusted "fairway" just north of Badwater Basin. The knee-high salt formations grow slowly as shallow groundwater below Devils Golf Course is drawn upward by capillary action. Rarely, a salt spring, where saline groundwater naturally comes to the surface, will open up at Devils Golf Course. Though the surface area of the springs is seldom scarcely larger than a bathtub, their salty depths can be mesmerizing.

Visitors are advised to avoid trekking out on the salt flats near Badwater in summer when daytime temperatures rise well over 120 degrees Fahrenheit, but fortunately a geologic point of interest can be viewed from the Badwater parking lot. Precambrian rocks that form the cliff adjacent to Badwater are approximately 1.7 billion years old, some of the oldest in California. The mottled browns and blacks of the cliff face are so contorted that it's difficult to determine what type of rock they were before they were metamorphosed to gneiss, uplifted, and eroded to form the cliff face seen today. Only about 11 million years ago, magma intruded into the Precambrian rocks, forming the Willow Spring Pluton, a dark-colored igneous rock of diorite to gabbro composition. It blends in well with the Precambrian rocks.

A small spring at Badwater, the low point in Death Valley

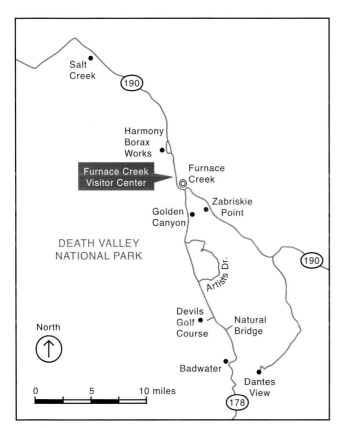

The surface of the salt flat at Badwater, smoothed by water during rare high rainfall events

For thousands of years, the creeks draining the surrounding mountains have carried sediment and salt-laden water down to the valley floor, where a mixture of mud and mineral salts accumulated. This mineral slurry was dug up and processed to extract borate at Harmony Borax Works, the largest borax mining operation in Death Valley in the 1880s, located just north of Furnace Creek. A short interpretive trail through the original borax refining operation details the history of borate mining in Death Valley.

Due to the considerable expense of hauling anything out of Death Valley, Harmony Borax Works was established to process the raw material. Refining the borax was a technically simple but labor-intensive process. First, the mud and salt mixture was mixed with boiling water. Carbonated soda was added to the mix, which caused the borax to dissolve and the mud and lime to settle out to the bottom of the vat. The borax-saturated liquid was drawn off to another tank, where the borax crystallized on metal rods. Finally, the crystallized borax was chipped off the metal rods and transported by the iconic twenty-mule-team wagon trains out of Death Valley to the nearest railroad. The work was hellish and continued year-round, even though it was too hot during summer for the borate to crystallize.

Golden Canyon

At Golden Canyon, just south of Furnace Creek, you can take an interpretive trail that goes into the canyon, cutting through ancient alluvial fans and lakebeds. A trail guide lists ten points of interest extending about a mile up the canyon, where you can see how ancient lakebeds and alluvial fans of the 6-million-year-old Furnace Creek Formation were deposited. The alluvial fans extended down into a valley with a lake. When lake levels were high, their water overlapped onto bordering alluvial fans, so lake sediments were deposited atop the

Wagon train at Harmony Borax Works

Ripples on lake-deposited sedimentary rock in Golden Canyon

Red Cathedral in Golden Canyon

alluvium. As lake levels dropped, the alluvial fans extended over the lake sediments. At stop 6, you can see delicate ripple marks weaving an intricate pattern on the top of a rock layer. The ripples formed in the sediment of a shallow windswept lake. The depositional sequence was later tilted, uplifted, and cut by flash floods and is now exposed in the canyon walls. The Golden Canyon trail ends at the massive cliff face of Red Cathedral, an iron-rich, erosion-resistant sedimentary rock.

Artists Drive

The confluence of rock type, weathering, and erosion created the striking beauty of the rugged landscape along 9-mile-long Artists Drive. From the yellow of limonite to the brick red of hematite, various iron oxides in the Artists Drive Formation create an entire palette of colors. Mixed in with gravel and lakebed deposits are thick sequences of volcanic ash, erupted from nearby volcanoes in Miocene time. The volcanic ash is frequently buff to gray but can also weather to pale green hues.

Artists Drive Formation

62. MOJAVE NATIONAL PRESERVE
Sand Dunes and Volcanic Tuff

Mojave National Preserve encompasses a large, geologically diverse landscape with forms ranging from cinder cones, sand dunes, and caves to mountains of granite and buttes of volcanic tuff. Kelso Dunes formed during at least five growth spurts in the past 25,000 years. As the climate has cyclically heated and cooled during that time, Soda Lake, located 20 miles northwest of Kelso Dunes, has been alternately flooded and dry. Sand grains, blown preferentially to the southeast when Soda Lake is dry, built up over millennia to form Kelso Dunes. Vegetation has stabilized the lower part of the dunes and provides a rich habitat for fringe-toed lizards, kangaroo rats, and kit foxes, all of which leave tracks in the sand. Today, a hike to the top of the 600-foot dunes offers a rewarding panoramic view of the surrounding desert and a chance to hear the "singing sands" on the hike down the dune face. A poorly understood mechanism involving friction between sand grains causes a booming sound on steep faces.

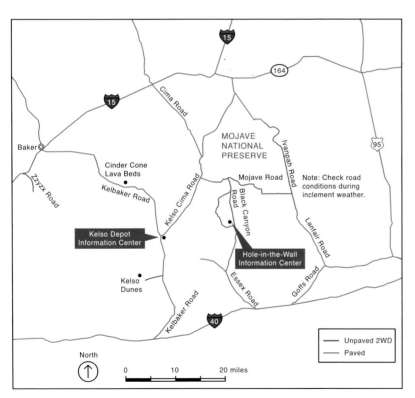

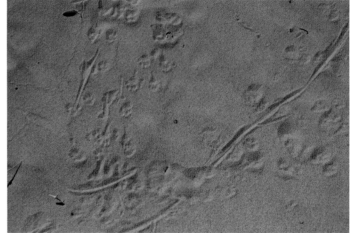

Animal tracks in the Kelso Dunes

Hole-in-the-Wall, near the center of Mojave National Preserve, is tucked into the base of a butte of tuff, a hard rock composed of volcanic ash and rock fragments. The tuff was the fallout from a massive volcanic eruption nearly 19 million years ago from the Woods Mountains, east of Hole-in-the-Wall. A short, 1.5-mile loop trail circumnavigates the butte and includes the popular "ring trail," a narrow cleft in the rocks in which bolted iron rings serve as handholds and footholds for hikers. The tuff looks like Swiss cheese because holes, including the actual "hole-in-the-wall," have eroded into it.

Petroglyphs on volcanic tuff near Hole-in-the-Wall at Mojave National Preserve

Hole-in-the-Wall, a butte of volcanic tuff

63. JOSHUA TREE NATIONAL PARK
Rock Weathering

Joshua Tree National Park is a twofer. Visitors get not one, but two deserts—the lower-elevation Colorado Desert and the higher-elevation Mojave. Creosote and cactus inhabit the Colorado Desert, while the higher and wetter Mojave is home to the infamous Joshua Tree, which John Frémont, an early explorer to the region, described as "the most repulsive tree in the vegetable Kingdom."

The Hidden Valley and Jumbo Rocks Campgrounds are popular places to explore the park's weathered granitic rocks. The dominant minerals are light-colored feldspars and quartz, but weathering can give these rock a golden hue. The granitic rock at Joshua Tree began weathering when it was still underground, as water infiltrating from the surface worked its way into fractures in the rock, slowly altering some of its minerals to clay. Through time, erosion removed the overlying weathered rock, including the weathered material along the cracks, exposing the hard granitic rock. The orientation of the original fractures, called joints, drives the shape of the outcrops. Extensive weathering along at least three intersecting sets of joints, oriented horizontally and vertically, created the rounded blocks at Joshua Tree National Park.

Dikes are common features of granitic rocks and are particularly well represented in Joshua Tree National Park. The dikes look like white or light-colored lines that crisscross each other in outcrops, but they extend deep into the rock. Inches to feet in width, the dikes formed from molten magma that pushed into fractures in the granitic rock while it was still cooling deep underground. The magma that formed the dike was much richer in the light-colored minerals quartz and potassium feldspar than that of the surrounding rock, giving the dikes a lighter color. The quartz and feldspar crystals in many of the dikes are larger toward the center of the dike, the result of different rates of cooling. As molten magma enters a rock fracture, it chills quickly at the margins, so only small crystals can form. The magma on the interior of the dike cools more slowly, allowing larger crystals to form.

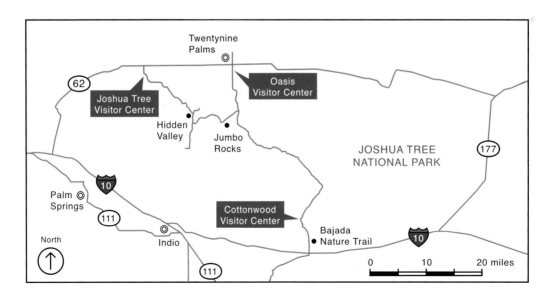

Pinto gneiss (the dark rocks on the mountaintop), intruded by the light granitic rock below it at Joshua Tree National Park

Weathered granitic rock at the Jumbo Rocks Campground in Joshua Tree National Park

64. SALTON SEA STATE RECREATION AREA
A Saline Lake

The Salton Sea, California's largest saline lake, formed accidentally in 1905 when Colorado River floodwaters breached a temporary water diversion structure and flowed unabated into the Salton Trough for almost two years. Although the 1905 flood was caused by humans, it duplicated previous natural floods that have occurred over thousands of years. The Colorado River, which normally flows south into the Gulf of California, deposits a delta of sediment at its mouth. When the delta gets too elevated, the Colorado River turns northward into the Salton Trough, forming an inland sea. Eventually, the delta erodes sufficiently that the river returns to its normal southward course and the sea evaporates. Evaporation is surprisingly rapid. In the early 1500s, the Salton Sea was 200 feet higher than it is today, but by the time the explorer Juan Bautista de Anza crossed in 1774, it was nothing but a dry, salty lakebed.

Today, the dominant inflow to the Salton Sea is agricultural runoff from farms in the Coachella Valley to the north and the Imperial Valley to the south. The runoff contributes to problems with nutrient loading, algae blooms, and fish die-offs. During most years, the rate of evaporation is greater than precipitation and agricultural runoff combined, so the Salton Sea has been shrinking for decades. As the water evaporates, salts are left behind; this has increased the Salton Sea's salinity from less than one part per thousand in 1905 to 44 parts per thousand today. For comparison, the salinity of seawater is about 35 parts per thousand.

With its base more than 200 feet below sea level, the Salton Trough is almost as low as Death Valley. The San Andreas Fault bounds its northeast side and the San Jacinto Fault its southwest side. The Gulf of California, 115 miles south of the Salton Sea, exists because it lies on a divergent plate boundary, a spreading zone at the northern end of the East Pacific Rise. The Salton Trough is also spreading, and although it is not yet a mid-ocean ridge within a spreading zone, the crust is thin here too. Wells at a geothermal field at the southern end of the Salton Sea tap into superheated brine more than mile belowground. The steam runs turbines that produce over 300 megawatts of electricity, making the Salton Sea field one of California's most important geothermal resource areas.

The Salton Sea

65. ANZA-BORREGO DESERT STATE PARK
Flash Floods

Anza-Borrego's diverse desert ecosystem is home to bighorn sheep, roadrunners, and golden eagles, but the park is most famous for vast carpets of early spring wildflowers. At 600,000 acres, the park encompasses diverse geology as well. The Narrows Earth Trail, a short half-mile loop from California 78 in the center of Anza-Borrego, has an information pamphlet available at the trailhead discussing geologic features, including several different rock types, offsetting along a small earthquake fault, and the effects of flash floods.

The Borrego Palm Canyon Nature Trail, a 1.5-mile hike to an oasis of palm trees, winds gently through a boulder-studded wash that testifies to the power of flash floods. Although flash floods are seasonal, fueled by summer thunderstorms, the spring-fed stream in Palm Canyon flows year-round.

Flash floods can happen anywhere but are especially common in mountainous desert environments where there is little soil or vegetation to absorb the water. The rock and sediment slurry charges downslope within the walls of a canyon, but when it reaches the flat valley floor where the water is no longer confined, the muck is abruptly and unceremoniously dumped. During the next flash flood, the rock slurry flows out of the canyon in a slightly different direction, circumventing the previous deposit since water always seeks the lowest level. With time, the side-to-side deposition forms an alluvial fan, with the apex of the fan at the mouth of the canyon. Where canyons are closely spaced and runoff is high, alluvial fans overlap each other, forming a bajada (Spanish for "slope"), a group of coalescing alluvial fans.

Wildflowers blooming after rainwater accumulated on the valley floor, forming mudflats

Boulders deposited by flash floods along Borrego Palm Canyon Nature Trail

97

GLOSSARY

accretion. In plate tectonics, the mechanism by which material is added to the continent along a subduction zone boundary. Material from the subducting plate is scraped off onto the continent, forming an **accretionary wedge**.

alluvial fan. Fan-shaped sedimentary deposit at the mouth of a canyon, typically in desert environments.

alluvium. Sediment deposited by water.

amphibolite. A metamorphic rock composed principally of the minerals amphibole and plagioclase.

andesite. A volcanic rock intermediate in composition between iron-rich basalt and silica-rich rhyolite.

anthracite. The highest grade of coal, with a carbon content of 92 to 98 percent.

basalt. A dark-colored, iron- and magnesium-rich volcanic rock. Also called lava. Chemically equivalent to the intrusive igneous rock gabbro.

batholith. A large area (greater than 40 square miles) of granite or related intrusive igneous rocks.

bedding. General term for layers of sedimentary rock.

biotite. Black or dark brown mica, a mineral that breaks apart in flat sheets.

bituminous coal. Medium-quality coal, with a carbon content of 60 to 80 percent.

blueschist. A high-pressure, low-temperature metamorphic rock typically formed in a subduction zone.

boulder. A rock, typically rounded, with a diameter larger than 10 inches.

breccia. A rock type composed of very coarse angular fragments.

calcite. A mineral made of calcium carbonate ($CaCO_3$). The principal mineral in limestone.

caldera. A large volcanic depression formed from the collapse of land following a large volcanic eruption.

carbonic acid. An acid (H_2CO_3) formed from the interaction between water (H_2O) and carbon dioxide (CO_2) in soil and the atmosphere. The primary acid that dissolves limestone to create solution caves.

chert. Microcrystalline quartz. See **radiolarian chert.**

clay. A particle with a grain size smaller than $1/256$ millimeters, or a type of sediment composed primarily of clay particles.

claystone. A sedimentary rock composed of clay particles.

coal. A carbon-rich sedimentary rock that can burn.

cobble. A rock, typically rounded, with a diameter between 2.5 and 10 inches.

concretion. A typically spherical or egg-shaped feature in sedimentary rocks that is harder than the surrounding rock.

conglomerate. A sedimentary rock that includes rounded gravel or cobbles in a sandy matrix.

continental slope. In oceanography, the sloped transition between the relatively flat continental shelf and the ocean floor.

convergent. A type of plate tectonic boundary where one plate collides with another.

crossbed, crossbedding. In sedimentary rock, sets of thin layers of sand that are oblique to layers below. Crossbedding typically indicates movement of grains by water or wind.

crust (Earth's). The outer layer of the Earth, above the core and mantle. Oceanic crust is typically 3 to 6 miles thick, and continental crust ranges from approximately 20 to 30 miles thick, with a few places (e.g., Himalayas) exceeding 40 miles in thickness.

dacite. A volcanic rock intermediate in composition between andesite and rhyolite. Chemically equivalent to the intrusive igneous rock granodiorite.

differential weathering. Uneven rock surface caused by the more rapid weathering action by water, wind, and biota on the softer parts of a rock.

dike. Igneous intrusion of magma into cracks within existing rock.

diorite. A gray to dark gray intrusive igneous rock intermediate in composition between iron-rich gabbro and silica-rich granite. Chemically equivalent to the volcanic rock andesite.

dip. Maximum tilt, measured from horizontal, in rock layers.

divergent. A tectonic plate boundary where plates move away from each other (spreading center).

exfoliation. "Onion-skin" type weathering, common in granitic rocks.

extrusive igneous rock. A volcanic rock solidified from lava extruded on Earth's surface.

fanglomerate. A sedimentary deposit associated with an alluvial fan.

fault. Fracture along which movement has occurred.

feldspar. A common silicate mineral in igneous rocks. Two common feldspar groups are orthoclase (potassium feldspars) and plagioclase (sodium-calcium feldspars).

flash flood. Rapid rise in water caused by an inability of the ground to absorb precipitation. Commonly associated with storms in desert areas.

gabbro. An iron- and magnesium-rich intrusive igneous rock, chemically equivalent to the volcanic rock basalt.

geothermal. Relating to the heat of the Earth's interior.

gneiss. A metamorphic rock with alternating light and dark bands.

graded bedding. A type of sedimentary rock layering that grades from coarse particles below to finer particles above.

granite. A light-colored, silica-rich intrusive igneous rock, chemically equivalent to the volcanic rock rhyolite.

granitic. Granite and closely associated rocks, a term loosely used for light-colored intrusive igneous rocks that are rich in silica, including the mineral quartz.

granodiorite. An intrusive igneous rock that contains a nearly equal mix of light minerals (feldspar, quartz) and dark minerals (biotite, amphibole), typically with a salt-and-pepper appearance.

gravel. Particle size larger than sand, but smaller than cobbles, approximately 0.08 to 2.5 inches in diameter.

graywacke. Grayish sandstone with grains of various sizes, often deposited by turbidity currents. In California, it's the principal sandstone associated with the Franciscan Complex.

greenstone. An informal name for metamorphosed basalt. The green color is from the minerals chlorite, hornblende, and epidote.

hematite. A mineral (Fe_2O_3) that is the principal ore of iron.

hornblende. A mineral in the amphibole group.

hot spring. A thermal spring with a water temperature greater than 98 degrees Fahrenheit.

hydraulic mining. A gold mining method that uses water cannons to excavate placer deposits.

hydrothermal. Relating to mineral-rich hot water solution.

igneous rock. Rock that was originally molten, including extrusive igneous (volcanic) and intrusive igneous (plutonic) rocks.

interbedded. Alternating sedimentary layers, such as a shale-sandstone-shale sequence.

intrusive igneous rock. Igneous rock that solidifies from magma deep underground. Slow cooling results in larger crystals than those formed in extrusive igneous (volcanic) rocks.

lava. Molten rock that erupts from a volcano. Also, the same material after it is solidified.

lignite. The lowest grade of coal, with a carbon content of approximately 60 percent.

limestone. A sedimentary rock composed of calcium carbonate ($CaCO_3$).

limonite. A brown rock consisting of iron-rich minerals.

magma. Molten rock found below the Earth's surface.

mantle. The layer of Earth that is between the core and the crust.

marble. Metamorphic limestone or dolomite.

marine terrace. An elevated, wave-cut platform exposed by uplift along a seacoast or lowered sea level.

matrix. The smaller material type that encompasses a larger or more significant object, such as cobblestones in a sandy matrix, or a clam fossil in a mudstone matrix.

mélange. A mixture of different rock types.

metamorphic rock. Rock that has been altered by changes in temperature and pressure.

mudstone. A fine-grained sedimentary rock composed of clay- and silt-size particles.

normal fault. An extensional fault where the upper (hanging) wall of the fault moves downward with respect to the lower (foot) wall.

olivine. A green mineral that is common in dark igneous rocks such as basalt, gabbro, and peridotite.

ophiolite. A sequence of mantle and oceanic crustal rocks indicative of subduction zone tectonics.

peat. Partially decayed marshy plant material that can ignite when dry.

pebbles. Alternate name for gravel.

peridotite. Dense igneous rock consisting of the minerals pyroxene and olivine.

petrified wood. Wood in which the cellular structure has been replaced by silica.

pillow basalt. Basalt lava that erupts underwater, forming pillow-shaped blobs.

placer deposit. Gold-bearing gravel deposit.

plagioclase. A common light-colored, rock-forming mineral of the feldspar group.

plankton. Microscopic drifting organisms, either plant (phytoplankton) or animal (zooplankton), that live in water.

plate tectonics. A theory that explains how and why plates move on the surface of the Earth.

Pleistocene. The geologic epoch from 1.8 million to 11,500 years ago.

pluton. A body of intrusive igneous rock, such as granite.

potassium feldspar. A common, light-colored mineral in igneous rocks. Also called K-spar and orthoclase.

pyroxene. A dark mineral common in igneous rocks.

quartz. Silicon dioxide (SiO_2), the most common mineral.

quartz diorite. An intrusive igneous rock similar to granite.

radiolarian chert. Microcrystalline quartz formed from the silica-rich remains of radiolaria, a type of microscopic marine animal (zooplankton).

red bed. A reddish sedimentary rock layer, typically sandstone or shale. The red color is caused by the oxidation of iron-rich minerals.

reservoir rock. A permeable rock such as sandstone or limestone that serves as a reservoir for oil or gas.

reverse fault. A compressional fault where rock on one side of the fault moves up and over rock on the other side.

rhyolite. A light-colored, silica-rich volcanic rock. The extrusive equivalent of granite.

salinity. The salt content of water, typically expressed in parts per thousand. Seawater is approximately 35 parts per thousand.

sand. Sedimentary particles between $1/16$ and 2 millimeters in diameter.

sandstone. Rock composed of sand grains, predominantly quartz.

sea stack. A coastal steep-sided rocky feature that rises above sea level.

sediment. Material, such as gravel, sand, or mud, deposited by water or wind.

sedimentary rock. Rock solidified from sediment deposited by water, wind, or ice.

serpentinite. A rock, usually altered peridotite and related rocks from the upper mantle, composed of serpentine minerals.

shale. Sedimentary rock composed of very thin layers of clay- and silt-size particles.

silica. Silicon dioxide (SiO_2), the chemical formula of quartz.

silt. Sedimentary particles between 1/256 and 1/16 millimeter in diameter. Particle size smaller than sand, but larger than clay.

siltstone. Fine-grained sedimentary rock composed primarily of silt-size particles.

slate. A metamorphic fine-grained rock that breaks apart in flat sheets.

slickens. Outwash from hydraulic mining activities.

spreading center. A divergent tectonic plate boundary.

spring. A natural flow of groundwater to the Earth's surface.

stratovolcano. A large volcano built of alternating layers of lava and airborne material such as volcanic ash.

strike-slip fault. A fault in which the movement is primarily horizontal.

subduction zone. A type of convergent plate tectonic boundary in which oceanic crust of one plate is moving beneath another plate.

submarine fan. A fan-shaped deposit at the mouth of a submarine canyon.

tafoni. A type of rock weathering resulting in a pitted surface.

tonalite. A type of granitic rock.

trace fossil. Fossilized evidence of animal activity, such as a burrow, footprint, or feces.

transform fault. A plate tectonic boundary where crust is neither created nor destroyed. The plates simply move past each other.

tsunami. A large wave or series of waves caused by large-scale water displacement, such as from an undersea earthquake.

tufa. Calcium carbonate rock formed from the interaction of calcium-rich springwater and carbonate-rich lake water.

tuff. A rock composed of very small (less than 0.2 inches in diameter) volcanic rock fragments.

turbidite. A rock formed from underwater turbidity current deposit.

turbidity current. Underwater gravity flow that transports sediment rapidly downslope, sometimes referred to as an "underwater landslide."

weathering. The action of water, wind, plants, bacteria, and temperature change that serve to break down rock into progressively smaller particles, eventually creating soil.

SITE CONTACT INFORMATION

Northeast California

1. Lava Beds National Monument
   www.nps.gov/labe
   (530) 667-8100

2. Mount Shasta
   USFS Shasta-Trinity National Forest
   www.fs.fed.us/r5/shastatrinity
   (530) 226-2500

3. Castle Crags State Park
   www.parks.ca.gov
   (530) 235-2684

4. McArthur–Burney Falls
   Memorial State Park
   www.parks.ca.gov
   (530) 335-2777

5. Lassen Volcanic National Park
   www.nps.gov/lavo
   (530) 595-4444

North Coast

6. Jedediah Smith Redwoods State Park
   www.parks.ca.gov
   (707) 458-3018

7. Crescent City/Redwood National
   Park Visitor Center
   www.nps.gov/redw
   (707) 464-6101

8. Patrick's Point State Park
   www.parks.ca.gov
   (707) 677-3570

9. Cache Creek Natural Area
   BLM Ukiah Field Office
   www.blm.gov/ca/st/en/fo/ukiah/
   cachecreek.html
   (707) 468-4000

10. Salt Point State Park
    www.parks.ca.gov
    (707) 847-3221

San Francisco Bay Area

11. Sonoma Coast State Park
    www.parks.ca.gov
    (707) 875-3483

12. Calistoga's Petrified Forest
    www.petrifiedforest.org
    (707) 942-6667

13. Napa Valley
    No suitable contact information

14. Point Reyes National Seashore
    www.nps.gov/pore
    (415) 464-5100

15. Golden Gate National
    Recreation Area
    www.nps.gov/goga
    (415) 561-4700

16. Sibley Volcanic Regional Preserve
    www.ebparks.org/parks/sibley
    (888) 327-2757

17. Black Diamond Mines
    Regional Preserve
    www.ebparks.org/parks/
    black _ diamond
    (925) 757-2620

18. Mount Diablo State Park
    www.parks.ca.gov
    (925) 837-2525

19. Vasco Caves Regional Preserve
    www.ebparks.org/parks/vasco
    (888) 327-2757

20. Mavericks Surf Break
    www.maverickssurf.com
    (415) 462-6200

21. San Gregorio State Beach
    www.parks.ca.gov
    (650) 879-2170

22. Bean Hollow State Beach
    www.parks.ca.gov
    (650) 879-2170

23. Los Trancos Open Space Preserve
    www.openspace.org/preserves/
    pr _ los _ trancos.asp
    (650) 691-1200

24. Almaden Quicksilver County Park
    www.sccgov.org/portal/site/parks
    (408) 268-3883

Sierra Nevada

25. Sutter Buttes
    The Middle Mountain Foundation
    (the Sutter Buttes
    Regional Land Trust)
    www.middlemountain.org
    (530) 671-6116

26. Empire Mine State Historic Park
    www.parks.ca.gov
    (530) 273-8522

27. Malakoff Diggens State Historic Park
    www.parks.ca.gov
    (530) 265-2740

28. Mather Regional Park
    www.vernalpools.org/
    MatherSchedule.htm

29. Lake Tahoe
    www.fs.fed.us/r5/ltbmu/recreation/
    visitor-center
    USFS Taylor Creek Visitor Center
    (530) 543-2674

30. Grover Hot Springs State Park
    www.parks.ca.gov
    (530) 694-2248

31. California State Mining
    and Mineral Museum
    www.parks.ca.gov
    (209) 742-7625

32. Yosemite National Park
    www.nps.gov/yose
    (209) 372-0200

33. Kings Canyon National Park
    www.nps.gov/seki
    (559) 565-3341

34. Sequoia National Park
    www.nps.gov/seki
    (559) 565-3341

Eastern Sierra

35. Bodie State Historic Park
    www.parks.ca.gov
    (760) 647-6445

36. Mono Lake Tufa
    State Natural Reserve
    www.parks.ca.gov
    (760) 647-6331

37. Panum Crater
    www.monolake.org/visit/panum
    (760) 647-6595

38. Devils Postpile National Monument
    www.nps.gov/depo
    (760) 934-2289

39. Horseshoe Lake
    No suitable contact information

40. Hot Creek Geological Site
    Inyo National Forest
    www.fs.fed.us/r5/inyo
    (760) 873-2400

41. Convict Lake
    www.fs.fed.us/r5/inyo/recreation/
    camping/convict-lake.shtml
    (760) 873-2400

Central Coast

42. Castle Rock State Park
    www.parks.ca.gov
    (408) 867-2952

43. Natural Bridges State Beach
    www.parks.ca.gov
    (831) 423-4609

44. Carmel River State Beach
    www.parks.ca.gov
    (831) 649-2836

45. Point Lobos State Natural Reserve
    www.parks.ca.gov
    (831) 624-4909

46. Morro Bay State Park
    www.parks.ca.gov
    (805) 772-7434

47. Pinnacles National Monument
    www.nps.gov/pinn
    (831) 389-4485

South Coast

48. Gaviota State Park
    www.parks.ca.gov
    (805) 968-1033

49. Kern County Museum
    www.kcmuseum.org
    (661) 852-5000

50. Red Rock Canyon State Park
    www.parks.ca.gov
    (661) 231-4389

51. Santa Monica Mountains National
    Recreation Area
    www.nps.gov/samo
    (805) 370-2300

52. Vasquez Rocks Natural Area
    www.lacountyparks.org
    (661) 268-0840

53. Devils Punchbowl County Park
    www.devils-punchbowl.com
    (619) 944-2743

54. La Brea Tar Pits
    www.tarpits.org
    (323) 934-7243

55. Abalone Cove Shoreline Park
www.palosverdes.com/rpv/
recreationparks/
AbaloneCoveShoreline/index.cfm
(310) 377-1222

56. Crystal Cove State Park
www.parks.ca.gov
(949) 494-3539

57. San Onofre State Beach
www.parks.ca.gov
(949) 492-4872

58. Torrey Pines State Natural Reserve
www.parks.ca.gov
(858) 755-2063

59. Mission Trails Regional Park
www.mtrp.org
(619) 668-3281

60. Cuyamaca Rancho State Park
www.parks.ca.gov
(760) 765-3020

Deserts

61. Death Valley National Park
www.nps.gov/deva
(760) 786-3200

62. Mojave National Preserve
www.nps.gov/moja
(760) 252-6100

63. Joshua Tree National Park
www.nps.gov/jotr
(760) 367-5500

64. Salton Sea State Recreation Area
www.parks.ca.gov
(760) 393-3059

65. Anza-Borrego Desert State Park
www.parks.ca.gov
(760) 767-5311

FURTHER READING

Listed below are the primary documents, maps, and Web sites that provided the technical basis for the site summaries in *California Rocks!* These references are provided for readers who wish to delve deeper into the subject material for a specific site.

General Sources

Alt, D., and D. Hyndman. 2000. *Roadside Geology of Northern and Central California.* Mountain Press Publishing Company.

American Geological Institute. 1976. *Dictionary of Geological Terms.* Anchor Press.

Glazner, A., and R. Sharp. 1993. *Geology Underfoot in Southern California.* Mountain Press Publishing Company.

Harden, D. 2004. *California Geology* (2nd edition). Pearson Education.

Norris, R., and R. Webb. 1990. *Geology of California* (2nd edition). John Wiley & Sons.

Sloan, D. 2006. *Geology of the San Francisco Bay Region.* University of California Press.

Whitney, J. 1865. *Geology. Volume I. Report of the Progress and Synopsis of the Field-Work from 1860 to 1864.* Geological Survey of California. Caxton Press of Sherman & Co.

Technical Sources

Aalto, K. R. 1989. Geology of Patrick's Point State Park, Humboldt County, California. *California Geology* 42:125–133.

Clifton, H. E., and G. W. Hill. 1987. Paleocene Submarine Canyon Fill, Point Lobos, California. In M. L. Hill, ed. *Geological Society of America Centennial Field Guide, Cordilleran Region,* pp. 239–244.

Dibblee, T. W., Jr. 1988. *Geology of the Solvang-Gaviota Quadrangles.* Dibblee Geological Foundation, Map DF-16.

Elder, W. P. 2001. Geology of the Golden Gate Headlands. In P. W. Stoffer and L. C. Gordon, eds., *Geology and Natural History of the San Francisco Bay Area: A Field-Trip Guidebook,* U.S. Geological Survey Bulletin 2188, pp. 61–86.

Farrar, C. D., W. C. Evans, D. Y. Venezky, S. Hurwitz, and L. K. Oliver. 2007. *Boiling Water at Hot Creek: The Dangerous and Dynamic Thermal Springs in California's Long Valley Caldera.* U.S. Geological Survey Fact Sheet 2007-3045.

Grantz, A. 1976. Sandstone Caves (Tafoni) in the Central Santa Cruz Mountains, San Mateo County. *California Geology* 29:51–54.

Greene, D. C., and C. H. Stevens. 2002. *Geologic Map of Paleozoic Rocks in the Mount Morrison Pendant, Eastern Sierra Nevada, California.* California Division of Mines and Geology Map Sheet 53.

Hausback, B. P., and T. H. Nilsen. 1999. Sutter Buttes. In Wagner, D. L., and S. A. Graham, eds., *Geologic Field Trips in Northern California.* California Division of Mines and Geology Special Publication 119, pp. 246–254.

Huber, N. K. 1989. *The Geologic Story of Yosemite National Park.* U.S. Geological Survey Bulletin 1595.

John, D. A. 2001. Miocene and Early Pliocene Epithermal Gold-Silver Deposits in the Northern Great Basin, Western United States. *Economic Geology* 96:1827–1853.

Kane, P. 2002. Burney Falls . . . One of a Kind: A Brief Geology of Burney Falls. McArthur–Burney Falls Memorial State Park brochure.

Kennedy, M. P., and S. S. Tan. 2005. *Geologic Map of the San Diego 30′ x 60′ Quadrangle.* California Geological Survey.

Mattison, E. 1990. California's Fossil Forest, Sonoma County. *California Geology* 43:195–202.

Monterey Bay Aquarium Research Institute. 2005. *A History Lesson from Monterey Canyon.* Annual report.

Morton, D. M. 2004. *Preliminary Digital Geologic Map of the Santa Ana 30′ x 60′ Quadrangle.* California Geologic Survey Open File Report 99-172.

Shlemon, R. J. 1987. The Cristianitos Fault and Quaternary Geology, San Onofre State Beach, California. In M. L. Hill, ed. *Geological Society of America Centennial Field Guide, Cordilleran Section*, pp. 171–174.

Stoffer, P. W. 2005. *The San Andreas Fault in the San Francisco Bay Area, California: A Geology Fieldtrip Guidebook to Selected Stops on Public Lands.* U.S. Geological Survey Open-File Report 2005-1127.

Sullivan, R., and J. Waters. 1980. Mount Diablo Coalfield. *California Geology* 33:51–59.

Swinchatt, J., and D. Howell. 2004. *The Winemaker's Dance: Exploring Terroir in the Napa Valley.* University of California Press.

Todd, V. R. 2004. *Preliminary Geologic Map of the El Cajon 30´ x 60´ Quadrangle, Southern California.* U.S. Geological Survey Open-File Report 2004-1361.

Trent, D. D. 1998. Geology of Joshua Tree National Park. *California Geology* 51:3–15.

Vennum, W. 1994. Geology of Castle Crags, Shasta and Siskiyou Counties. *California Geology* 47:31–38.

Whistler, D. P. 1987. *Field Guide to the Geology of Red Rock Canyon and the Southern El Paso Mountains, Mojave Desert, California.* NAGT Guidebook, Far Western Section.

Yerkes, R. F., and R. H. Campbell. 2005. *Preliminary Geologic Map of the Los Angeles 30´ x 60´ Quadrangle, Southern California.* U.S. Geological Survey Open-File Report 2005-1019.

Web Sites with Geologic Information

Crystal Cave in Sequoia National Park: www.sequoiahistory.org/cave/cave.htm.

Death Valley National Park: http://geomaps.wr.usgs.gov/parks/deva/devaft.html.

Devils Postpile: http://geomaps.wr.usgs.gov/parks/depo/dpgeol1.html.

Devils Punchbowl: www.devils-punchbowl.com/pages/geology.html

Horseshoe Lake: http://lvo.wr.usgs.gov/CO2.html.

Kern County Museum: www.kcmuseum.org.

La Brea Tar Pits: www.tarpits.org

Lake Tahoe: http://tahoe.usgs.gov/facts.html.

Lassen Volcanic National Park: www.nps.gov/lavo/naturescience/eruption_lassen_peak.htm.

Lava Beds National Monument: http://vulcan.wr.usgs.gov/Volcanoes/MedicineLake/framework.html.

Mather Vernal Pools: www.sacvalleycnps.org/Conservation/vernalpools/mather3.htm.

Mavericks Surf Break: http://sanctuarysimon.org/monterey/sections/other/whats_new_mavericks.php.

Mono Lake: www.monolake.org/visit/vc.

Mount Diablo: www.mdia.org.

Mount Shasta: http://vulcan.wr.usgs.gov/Volcanoes/Shasta/framework.html.

Panum Crater: http://vulcan.wr.usgs.gov/LivingWith/VolcanicPast/Notes/panum_crater.html.

Salt Point State Park: www.fortrossstatepark.org/saltpointfiledguidegeology.htm.

Torrey Pines State Natural Reserve: www.torreypine.org/geology/geology.html.

U.S. Bureau of Land Management. Rockhounding. www.blm.gov/ca/st/en/fo/needles/rock.html.

U.S. Geological Survey. San Francisco Bay Region Geology. http://geomaps.wr.usgs.gov/sfbay/index.html.

U.S. Geological Survey. *This Dynamic Earth: The Story of Plate Tectonics.* Book available online at http://pubs.usgs.gov/gip/dynamic/dynamic.html#anchor4161180.

U.S. Geological Survey. Volcano Hazards Program. Current Alert: http://volcano.wr.usgs.gov/vhpstatus.php.

U.S. National Park Service. Tour of Park Geology.: www.nature.nps.gov/geology/parks/bystate.cfm#ca.

INDEX

Abalone Cove landslide, 79
Abalone Cove Shoreline
  Park, 79
accretion, 13
accretionary wedge, 3, 13,
  17, 30
Agate Beach, 16
agricultural runoff, 96
Alegria Formation, 71
alluvial fans, 76, 87, 90, 97
alluvium, 81
Almaden Quicksilver County
  Park, 39
Alpine County, 46
Amargosa Range, 87
amphibolite, 42
andesite, 5, 7, 41, 46, 69, 74
anemones, 27
animal tracks, 19
anticline, 72
Anza-Borrego Desert State
  Park, 97
arches, 21, 64
Arch Rock, 21
argillite, 61
Arroyo Olemus Loke, 24
Artists Drive, 91
Artists Drive Formation, 91
ash, volcanic, 11, 54, 57, 69,
  73, 79, 91
Aspen Meadow Formation, 61
assay office, 47

Badwater, 88–89
bajada, 97
barrier beach, 83
basalt, 2, 5, 6, 9; flows of,
  73, 74; ocean floor, 13, 14;
  pillow, 13, 14, 16, 29, 30,
  33, 74; vesicular, 31
basin, closed, 88
Basin and Range Province, x,
  4, 87, 88
Baulines Bay, 24
Bay Area, 20
Beach Trail, 82–83
Bean Hollow State Beach, 37
benitoite, 47
Big Bend, 70
Big Sur, 62
biotite, 52, 85
Black Diamond Coal Mine, 32
Black Diamond Mines
  Regional Preserve, 32
Black Diamond Vein, 32
blueschist, 16, 33; sea stack
  of, 21
Bodega Head, 21
Bodie State Historic Park, 55
boiling springs, 11
Bolinas Lagoon, 24
borate mining, 90
borax, 90
brea, 78
breccia, 69, 74
Bridalveil Fall, 48, 49

Bristol Lake, 88
Bumpass Hell, 11
Bumpass, Kendall
  Vanhook, 11
Burney Basalt, 9
Burney Falls, 9
burrows, fossils of, 18, 19, 36

Cache Creek Natural Area, 17
Cadiz Lake, 88
Calabasas Formation, 75
calcite, 16, 61
calcium carbonate, 37, 53,
  56, 63
California: state fossil, 78;
  state gemstone, 47; state
  rock, 13; state soil, 44
California State Mining and
  Mineral Museum, 47
Calistoga, 22
carbon dioxide, 59
Carmel Canyon, 65
Carmelo Formation, 26, 66
Carmel River State Beach, 65
Cascade Range, volcanoes of,
  4, 5, 7, 10
Cascades Volcano
  Observatory, 7
Cascadia Subduction Zone, 15
Castle Crags State Park, 8
Castle Dome, 8
Castle Rock State Park, 63

Cathedral Peak
  Granodiorite, 51
caves: in basalt, 6; in marble,
  53; in sandstone, 34; sea,
  36; in talus, 69
Central Valley, 4
Ceremonial Rock, 16
channel deposits, 73, 76
Channel Islands, 74
Charmlee Wilderness Park, 75
chert, 16, 61; sea stack of, 21
Chiquito Peak Monzogranite,
  85
cinnabar, 39
Circle X Ranch, 74
Clairemont Mesa, 82
clams, fossils of, 83
Clark Vein, 32
clay, 79, 94
claypan, 44
claystone, 71, 76, 81
climate, changes in, 16, 80,
  88, 92
Coachella Valley, 96
coal, 32
Coast Ranges, x, 14, 30;
  formation of, 2, 3; mercury
  ore in, 39
Colorado Desert, x, 94
Colorado River, 96
columnar jointing, 58
composite volcano, 59
Concord Fault, 33

concretions, 34
Conejo Volcanics, 74
conglomerate, 25–26, 67, 73, 76, 84
continental drift. *See* plates, tectonic
convergent plate boundary, 2, 5, 70
Convict Lake, 61
coprolites, 19
core (Earth's), 1
Cornish pump, 42
Corona Heights, 29
Cowles Mountain, 84
crabs, burrows of, 36
Crescent City, 15
Cristianitos Fault, 81
crossbedding, 16, 82–83
crust (Earth's) 1; thinning of, 6, 87, 96
Crystal Cave, 53
Crystal Cove State Park, 80
Cuyamaca Gabbro, 85
Cuyamaca Mountains, 85
Cuyamaca Rancho State Park, 85

dacite, 7, 11, 46, 68, 69, 74; in a conglomerate, 84
Danby Lake, 88
Davidson, Mount, 29
Death Valley, 87, 88
Death Valley National Park, 88–91
Delmar Formation, 82, 83
delta, 96
deserts, 87
Devastated Area, 10
Devils Golf Course, 88

Devils Postpile National Monument, 58
Devils Punchbowl County Park, 77
Diablo, Mount, 33
diatoms, 71
differential weathering, 37, 63
dikes, 25, 75, 85, 94; sheeted, 14
diorite, 89
divergent plate boundaries, 1, 96
Domengine Formation, 32
Dove Spring Formation, 73
Drake, Sir Francis, 26–27
Drakes Beach, 26–27
Duxbury Reef, 27

Earth, structure of, 1
earthquakes, 13, 59; damage from, 24, 38; swarm of, 60; triggering of tsunamis, 15
East Bay Hills, 20, 31
East Pacific Rise, 96
El Capitan, 48
Empire Mine, 42
Empire Mine State Historic Park, 42
epithermal deposit, 55
erosion, 75, 94; by waves, 36, 64; of river valleys, 49
eruptions, volcanic, 7, 10–11, 22, 31, 54, 59, 70
evaporation, 96
exfoliation joints, 8, 50
extrusive igneous rocks, 2. *See also* andesite; basalt; dacite; lava; rhyolite

fairy shrimp, 44
fanglomerate, 76
Farallon Plate, 2–4, 40, 70; rocks of, 29, 30; subduction of, 13, 16, 20, 23, 33, 84
faults, 2, 3, 20, 33, 61, 77; gouge of, 36, 72; intrusions along, 68; sag ponds along, 38; scarps of, 87; trapping of oil by, 72; uplift along, 45, 46, 54, 87. *See also specific fault names*
feldspars, 25, 94. *See also* plagioclase; potassium feldspar
fining-up beds, 17, 65
fish, fossils of, 73
flash floods, 87, 97
Flat Rock, 83
floodplain deposits, 73
folds, 77
foliation, 75
forearc basin, 17
forty-niners, 43
fossils, 78, 83; mammals, 73; trace, 18, 19, 36
Franciscan Complex, 3, 13, 20, 33; mélange of, 16; pillow basalt of, 29; radiolarian chert of, 28
Frémont, John, 45, 94
Fricot Nugget, 47
fulgurites, 52
fumaroles, 11
Furnace Creek Formation, 90
fur traders, 9

gabbro, 14, 85, 89
Gaviota Formation, 71
Gaviota State Park, 71
gems, 47
geographic regions, x
geologic time, ix
geothermal field, 96
German Rancho Formation, 18–19
geysers, 60
ghost town, 55
glacial striations, 58
glaciers, 49
gneiss, 89, 95
Goat Buttes, 75
Goat Rock, 21
gold, 39, 47, 85; mining of, 42, 43, 47, 55, 85
Golden Canyon, 90–91
Golden Gate Fault, 24
Golden Gate Heights Park, 29
Golden Gate National Recreation Area, 28–30
Gorda Plate, 4, 5, 10, 13
graded bedding, 17, 37, 65
granitic rocks, 2, 3, 8, 24–25, 40, 84, 85, 94–95; minerals of, 52
granodiorite, 8, 25, 42, 50–51, 66–67, 84
Grass Valley District, 42
gravity flow, 65. *See also* turbidity current
graywacke, 13, 16, 33, 65; sea stack of, 21
Great Valley, x, 4
Great Valley sedimentary rocks, 20
Great Valley Sequence, 17
greenstone, 16, 33

ground sloths, 78
groundwater, 9, 46, 60, 88
Grover Hot Springs State
    Park, 46
Gulf of California, 96
Gulf of the Farallones
    National Marine
    Sanctuary, 27

Half Dome, 48, 50
Hamilton, Mount 33
hanging valleys, 49
hardpan, 44
hard rock mine, 42
Harmony Borax Works, 90
Hayward Fault, 31
hazards, geologic, 15
headlands, 16
hematite, 91
Hole-in-the-Wall, 93
hornblende, 52, 85
Horseshoe Lake, 59
Hot Creek, 60
Hot Creek Fish Hatchery, 60
hot springs, 11, 46, 54, 60
hydraulic mining, 43
hydrothermal areas, 10,
    11, 60

ice ages, 16, 45, 49, 78,
    80, 88
igneous rocks, 2
Imperial Valley, 96
interglacial periods, 16, 80
intrusive igneous rocks, 2, 8.
    See also diorite; gabbro;
    granitic rock; peridotite
iron oxides, 73, 76, 82, 91

Jedediah Smith Redwoods
    State Park, 14
joints, 8, 50, 58, 94
Josephine ophiolite, 14
Joshua Tree National Park,
    94–95
Juan Bautista de Anza, 96
Juan de Fuca Plate, 4, 5
Julian Schist, 85

Kearny Mesa, 82
Kehoe Beach, 25
Kelso Dunes, 92
Kern County Museum, 72
Kings Canyon National
    Park, 52
Kirker Fault, 33
Klamath Range, 14

La Brea Tar Pits, 72, 78
Laguna Coast Wilderness
    Park, 80
Laird Sandstone, 25
lakebeds, 88, 90
Lake Murray, 84
Lake Tahoe, 45
lake terraces, 45
landslides, 79, 81;
    underwater, 13, 17, 37, 67
Lassen Peak, 4, 5, 10–11
Lassen Volcanic National
    Park, 10–11
lava, 5, 6; caves in, 6; cooling
    of, 58; flows of, 9, 58;
    gas bubbles in, 31; silica
    content of, 7; tubes of, 6;
    underwater eruption of,
    13. See also basalt; rhyolite
Lava Beds National
    Monument, 6

Lavic Lake, 88
Lembert Dome, 50
lightning, 52
lignite, 32
limestone, 53, 56, 59, 72
limonite, 91
Linda Vista Formation, 82
lodgepole pine, 59
Lone Pine, 54
longshore drift, 65
Long Valley Caldera, 54, 60
Long Valley Observatory
    program, 59
Lookout Rock, 16
Los Angeles, diversion of
    water by, 56
Los Angeles County Natural
    History Museum, 73
Los Trancos Open Space
    Preserve, 38

magma, 2, 40; cooling of, 94;
    gas trapped in, 5; rising of,
    7; silica content of, 5
Malakoff Diggins State
    Historic Park, 43
Malibu Creek State Park, 75
mammals, fossils of, 73
Mammoth Crater, 6
Mammoth Mountain, 59
mammoths, 78
mantle, 1, 13; rock of, 14
marble, 53
Marin County, 28
marine terraces, 21, 64, 80
Marin Headlands, 28, 29
Mariposa, 47
Markleeville Center, 46
Marsh Creek Fault, 33
Marysville, 41, 43

Mather Regional Park, 44
Mavericks surf break, 35
McArthur–Burney Falls
    Memorial State Park, 9
McKittrick oil seep, 72
Medicine Lake Volcano, 5,
    6, 7
Mendocino Triple Junction, 31
Merced River, 49
mercury mine, 39
metamorphic rocks, 14, 16,
    23, 42, 75, 77, 85; of
    Sierra Nevada, 53, 61
metamorphism, 53
meteorites, 47
microclimates, 37, 63
Midpeninsula Regional Open
    Space District, 38
Millbrae, 38
minerals, 47; fluorescent, 47;
    iron-bearing, 71. See also
    specific mineral names
mineral salts, 90
mining: of borax, 90; of coal,
    32; of gold, 42, 43, 47,
    55, 85; hazards of, 32; of
    mercury, 39
Miocene fossils, 73
Mira Mesa, 82
Mission Trails Regional
    Park, 84
Mission Valley Formation, 84
Modoc Plateau, x, 5
Mojave Desert, x, 94
Mojave National Preserve,
    92–93
monarchs, 64
Monastery Beach, 65
Mono Crater chain, 57
Mono Lake, 56

Monterey Canyon, 65
Monterey Formation, 24, 25, 71, 80, 81
Monterey Peninsula, 67
Morro Bay State Park, 68
Morro Rock, 68
Mount Diablo Baseline, 33
Mount Diablo State Park, 33
Mount Morrison roof pendant, 61
Mount Morrison Sandstone, 61
mudflow, 10, 22
mud pots, 11
mudstone, 18, 19, 24, 27, 64
Muir, John, 49
Mushpot, 6

Napa Valley, 23
Native Americans, 9, 34, 45, 57
Natural Bridges State Beach, 64
Neenach, 69
New Almaden, 39
Nine Sisters, 68
1906 San Francisco earthquake, 24
normal faults, 3. *See also* faults
North American Plate, 2–4; accretion to, 29, 30; subduction beneath, 5, 10, 13, 15, 16, 20, 23, 40, 70; stretching of, 87; transform boundary along, 2, 17, 24
North Dome, 50

obsidian, 57
oil, 72; seeps of, 72; trap of, 72
olivine, 14, 85
ophiolite, 14, 33
Orange County, 80

Pacific Crest Trail, 8
Pacific Plate, 2, 3, 4, 13, 20, 24, 70
Palm Canyon, 97
Panamint Flat, 88
Panamint Range, 87
Panum Crater, 57
Paramount Ranch, 74
Patricks Point State Park, 16
peat, 32
Penasquitos Lagoon, 83
Peninsular Ranges, x, 84, 85; formation of, 2
peridotite, 8, 13, 14
Petrified Forest, 22
petrified wood, 22
phytoplankton, 71, 72
Pigeon Point Formation, 37
pillow basalt, 13, 14, 16, 29, 30, 33, 74
Pinnacles National Monument, 69
Piñon Fault, 77
placer deposits, 43
plagioclase feldspar, 11, 42, 52, 84, 85
plankton, 28, 61, 71, 72
plant, fossils of, 73
plates, tectonic, 1, 2; boundaries of, 1, 4, 31; theory of, 1. *See also* Farallon Plate; Gorda Plate; North American Plate; Pacific Plate

playas, 88
Pleistocene Ice Ages, 16, 45, 49, 78, 80, 88
Pluto, Mount 45
plutons, 40, 85, 89
Point Bonita, 29–30
Point Bonita Lighthouse, 29
Point Lobos, 26, 66–67
Point Lobos State Natural Reserve, 66–67
Point Mugu State Park, 74
Point Reyes, 20, 24–25
Point Reyes Conglomerate, 25–26, 67
Point Reyes Lighthouse, 25
Point Reyes National Seashore, 24–27
Portuguese Bend landslide, 79
Portuguese Tuff, 79
potassium feldspar, 51, 52, 67, 84, 85, 94
Pothole Dome, 51
potholes, 50
Precambrian rocks, 89
pumice, 57
Punchbowl Fault, 77
Punchbowl Formation, 77
Purisima Formation, 24, 26, 27, 36
Pyramid Lake, 45
pyroxene, 14

quartz, 22, 25, 52, 61, 85, 94; sand of, 32; veins of, 16, 42, 55
quartzite, 53

radiolaria, 13, 28
radiolarian chert, 13, 28–29, 33

rainfall: in the desert, 88; flooding of, 41, 44, 97; weathering by, 37, 53, 63
red beds, 71
Red Butte, 82
Red Rock, 29
Red Rock Canyon, 73
Red Rock Canyon State Park, 73
reef, 35, 80
reptiles, fossils of, 73
reverse fault, 25
rhyolite, 2, 5, 41, 57, 69; ash, 22; in a conglomerate, 84
Ricardo Group, 73
Richmond–San Rafael Bridge, 29
Rincon Formation, 71
ripple marks, 91
river deposits, 33
roche moutonnée, 50–51
rockfalls, 50
Rogers Lake, 88
roof pendants, 61
Round Top, 31
Round Top volcano, 31
Russian River, 21

saber-toothed cats, 73, 78
Sacate Formation, 71
Sacramento Valley; flooding of, 41
sag ponds, 38
Saint Helena, Mount, 22
Salinian Block, 20, 62, 66–67
salinity, 96
salt flats, 88–89
Salton Sea, 96
Salton Trough, 96
Salt Point State Park, 18–19

salts, 88, 89, 90
salt spring, 88
San Andreas Fault Zone, 2–4, 70; earthquakes along, 24, 38; folding and uplift along, 76, 77; northern end of, 31; southern end of, 96; transport of rocks along, 18–19, 20, 24, 26, 63, 67, 69
San Andreas Lake, 38
San Cristobal mine, 39
sand, 92; dunes of, 16, 21, 92; transport of, 65
sandbar, 83
San Diego County, 82, 84
sandstone, 13, 74, 76, 77; caves in, 34; concretions in, 34; crossbeds in, 82; graywacke, 13; iron oxide in, 82; of Great Valley Sequence, 17; of Monterey Formation, 80; tafoni in, 37, 63; trace fossils in, 36. See also Laird Sandstone; Mount Morrison Sandstone; Torrey Sandstone, Vaqueros Sandstone
San Francisco Bay Area, 20; earthquake of, 24, 38
San Francisco Peninsula, 20
San Francisquito Formation, 77
San Gabriel Mountains, 77
San Gregorio Fault, 24, 26, 35
San Gregorio State Beach, 36
San Jacinto Fault, 96
San Joaquin Hills, 80
San Joaquin soil, 44

San Joaquin Valley, 72
San Mateo, 37
San Mateo Formation, 81
San Onofre State Beach, 81
Santa Barbara County, 71
Santa Cruz Mountains, 63
Santa Cruz Mudstone, 24, 27, 64
Santa Lucia Granodiorite, 66
Santa Monica Mountains, 74
Santa Monica Mountains National Recreation Area, 74–75
Santa Monica Slate, 75
Santa Paula oil seep, 72
Santa Ynez Mountains, 71
Sawyer decision, 43
schist, 53, 85. See also blueschist
sea caves, 36
sea level, changes in, 16, 21, 71, 80
Searles Lake, 88
sea stacks, 16, 21; partially detached, 21; residual, 16
Sentinel Cave, 6
Sentinel Dome, 50
Sequoia National Park, 53
serpentine, 13
serpentinite, 13, 23, 42
Sespe Formation, 71
Sevehah Cliff, 61
shale, 16, 17, 23, 25, 33, 53, 67, 71, 75, 77
Shasta, Mount, 4, 5, 7; eruptions of, 7
Shastina, 7
sheeted dikes, 14
Sherwin Glaciation, 49
shield volcanoes, 7

Sibley Volcanic Regional Preserve, 31
Sierra Nevada, 40; formation of, 2; uplift of, 3, 40, 49, 54
Sierra Nevada Batholith, 40
silica: in hardpan, 44; in lava, 57; in magma, 5; in sedimentary rocks, 61, 71; replacement of wood by, 22; skeletons of, 13, 28
siltstone, 25, 27, 71, 76, 81, 82, 83
silver, 47
Siskiyou County, 7
Siskiyou Range, 14
Skull Cave, 6
slate, 75
slickens, 43
Smith River, 14
Soda Lake, 92
soil, 9, 23, 44, 59, 85
Solstice Canyon, 75
Sonoma coast, 18
Sonoma Coast State Park, 21
South Tufa, 56
spadefoot toads, 44
spreading zone, 1, 96
springs, 9, 46, 56, 60, 88
Squares Tunnel Formation, 61
Stadium Conglomerate, 84
stalactites, 53
stalagmites, 53
stamp mill, 55
state fossil, 78
state gemstone, 47
state rock, 13
state soil, 44
Stonewall Mine, 85
Stonewall Peak, 85

stratigraphic trap, 72
stratovolcanoes, 5, 7
streambeds, gold in, 43
Stump Beach, 18, 19
subduction, 2, 3, 4; earthquakes along, 15; of Gorda Plate, 5, 10, 13; heat generated by, 40, 61, 84; of Farallon Plate, 16, 17, 20, 23, 29; rocks metamorphosed in, 16
submarine canyons, 65, 67
submarine fan, 26, 61
Sunset Rocks, 21
surf breaks, 35
Sur-Nacimiento Fault, 66
Sutter Buttes, 41
syncline, 77

tafoni, 37, 63
Tahoe Basin, 45
talus caves, 69
tar, roofing, 78
Taylor Creek Visitor Center, 45
tectonic plates. See plate tectonics
Tehachapi Mountains, 70
tephra, 57
terraces: lake, 45; marine, 21, 64, 80
terroir, 23
Three Brothers, 50
tide pools, 27, 80
time, geologic, ix
Tioga Pass, 50
Tomales Bay, 24
tonalite, 25, 84
Topanga Formation, 75
Topanga State Park, 75

Torrey Pines State Natural Reserve, 82–83
Torrey Sandstone, 82–83
Townsends big-eared bats, 69
trace fossils, 19, 36, 67
transform boundary, 2, 31, 70
Transverse Ranges, x, 70, 74; formation of, 2, 3
tree die-off, 59
Trinity Peridotite, 8
triple junction, 4, 31
trondhjemite, 8
Truckee River, 45
tsunamis, 15
tufa towers, 56
tuff, 69, 74, 79, 92, 93; breccia 73
Tuolumne Meadows, 50–51
turbidite, 37, 65
turbidity currents, 13, 16, 17, 37, 65, 67
Twin Peaks, 29

unconformity, 82

Vaqueros Sandstone, 63, 71
Vasco Caves Regional Preserve, 34
Vasquez Formation, 76
Vasquez Rocks Natural Area, 76
veins, 16, 42, 55
vents, steam, 11
Ventura County, 72
vernal pools, 44

vesicles, 31, 73
viticulture, 23
volcanic ash, 11, 54, 57, 69, 73, 79, 91
volcanic breccia, 74
volcanoes: eruptions of, 7, 10–11, 22, 31, 54, 59, 70; plug of, 68; vent of, 7; young, 41, 57

water quality, 45
weathering: along joints, 8, 50; of granitic rock, 94; salt, 37, 63; along zones of weakness, 69, 71
Wedding Rock, 16
West Coast and Alaska Tsunami Warning Center, 15
Whitney, Josiah, 1, 23, 24, 78
Whitney, Mount, 54
wildflowers, 44, 97
Williams, Howell, 41
Willow Spring Pluton, 89
wind, 87
wine industry, 23
wollastonite, 61
Woods Mountains, 93
worms, burrows of, 19, 36

Yosemite National Park, 49–51
Yosemite Valley, 50

zooplankton, 28, 72

Katherine J. Baylor holds degrees in geology and geography from the University of California at Santa Barbara. She currently lives in the San Francisco Bay area and is a hydrogeologist for the U.S. Environmental Protection Agency. Kathy has traveled to over forty countries but always returns to California where she enjoys hiking, camping, and backpacking with her friends and family.